A POST CO. C

Sierra Nevada
Byways

Backcountry
drives for the whole
family

By **TONY HUEGEL**

Cover design, maps, art and production
by Jerry Painter

Photos by Tony Huegel
unless otherwise indicated

Caution

This book has been prepared to help you and your family enjoy safe backcountry driving. However, it is not intended to be an exhaustive resource on backcountry driving, nor is it intended to be your only resource. Also, you must understand that there are risks and dangers that are inevitable when driving in the backcountry.

This book is not an all–encompassing authority on the risks of backcountry driving. If you choose to drive in the backcountry, you assume all risks, dangers and liability that may result from your actions. The author and publisher of this book disclaim any and all liability for any injury, loss or damage that you, your passengers or your vehicle may incur.

Be safe. Exercise the caution and good judgment that visiting the backcountry demands. Bring the proper supplies. Be prepared for accidents, injuries, breakdowns or other misadventures, because help is almost always far away.

Copyright © 1994 by Tony Huegel.
Copies of this book can be ordered directly from the Post Register.
For information call (208) 522-1800;
P.O. Box 1800, Idaho Falls, Idaho 83403
ISBN 0-9636560-4-X
Made in the U.S.A.

Thanks

A number of people were key to bringing you this adventure travel guide. My wife, Lynn MacAusland, was more patient than I had a right to expect. My big brother, Peter, provided essential inspiration and counsel, as well as several photographs. Roger Plothow, once my boss, and Jerry Brady, my publisher, provided vital support and enthusiasm. Jerry Painter provided the talent and skill behind the graphics and design, as well as lots of sound advice. My editor, Mei-Mei Chan, contributed a great deal of hustle and support, and did an outstanding job editing the book. There also were a number of U.S. Forest Service employees who provided important information that helped make the book more complete, accurate and useful. And there was Dolora Marcoe, a friend and a kindred spirit who shared my craving for adventure, and left on the greatest adventure of all while I was on the road.

But no one provided more than my parents, Frank and Berdine Huegel, whose genes and upbringing are at the root of it all.

Cover photo: Catfish Lake, along the Bowman Lake Loop drive.

Contents

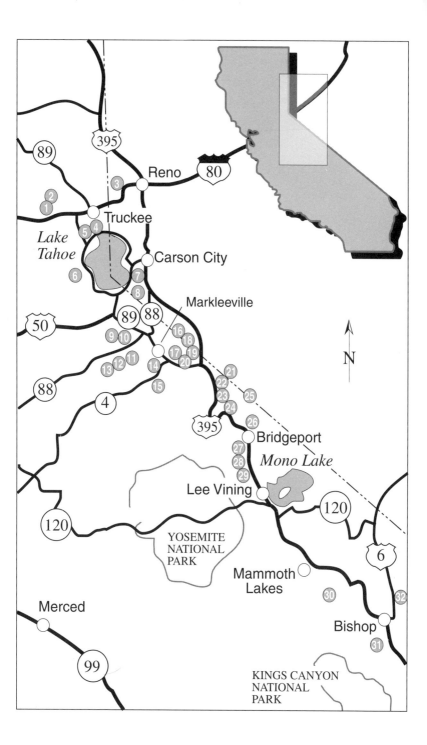

INTRODUCTION

Backcountry driving
in the Sierra Nevada

They stir the explorer in us all.

Anyone who has driven through California's Sierra Nevada Mountains has seen those tantalizing lines on the map, those dirt roads that branch off the highways and disappear into the mountains, canyons and forests of the largest single mountain range in the contiguous United States. Those roads, we think to ourselves as the asphalt miles roll by, are the ones we'd really like to be on.

Sierra Nevada Byways describes 32 backcountry drives through some of the best scenery that is accessible with a stock four-wheel drive vehicle.

They were chosen with the owners of sport-utility vehicles in mind, those legions of urban and suburban motorists, many with families, who've switched from sedans, vans and station wagons to rugged and versatile Ford Explorers, Jeep Cherokees, Nissan Pathfinders, Toyota 4Runners, Range Rovers and other such vehicles.

With a modern SUV, people don't need to hike long and arduous miles with packs on their backs to find solitude in pristine natural settings. It is now possible for a family to comfortably bypass crowded parks and road-ways and travel instead into rugged, magnificent backcountry settings where solitude abounds.

These rugged and well–appointed vehicles also allow seniors and dis-abled adventurers to experience remote areas that once seemed accessible only to serious four–wheelers, bikers and hikers.

My emphasis is on the crest of the Sierras, and the dramatic eastern slope. I love the elevation there, as well as the clean granite, autumn aspens, glacial valleys, sparkling lakes and exhilarating vistas. The gently sloping western side seems tame to me, with its population, its relatively well–watered forests and rolling grasslands. The east, in contrast, remains raw, wild and defiant. The descent and ascent rank among the steepest on the planet. The air that carries moisture across the western slope is dry by the time it crosses the crest, leaving the east less habitable for plants, ani-mals and humans alike. There, adventure, challenge and solitude abound.

The eastern side of the Sierra Nevada is a landscape of colliding geolog-ic and climactic forces, where the Mojave Desert and the Great Basin meet abruptly uplifted granitic mountains, glacial dumping grounds and volcanic moonscapes. They are young as mountains go, and are continuing to evolve. Their history has been read in rocks that are 440 million years old, although the mountains we see today began to form about 210 million years ago. In a single drive, you can go from a volcanic desert basin to a high–elevation landscape of meadows, streams and lakes fed by melting snow. You can see lava domes, ancient bristlecone pines and glaciers. You can climb and descend thousands of feet as you travel through broad valleys and deep canyons among some of the highest peaks in the lower 48 states.

Arranged basically from north to south, the drives extend from just north of Interstate 80 west of Reno, southward to the Tahoe and Mono basins, and the northern tip of the Owens Valley around Bishop. By no means are they all the great drives in the Sierras. Rather, they are a selection that will get you well–acquainted with the possibilities and on your way toward discovering more adventures on your own.

Driven with care, they are reasonably safe trips for a family in a factory-equipped 4x4. But backcountry travel, whether by foot, mountain bike or motorized vehicle, has risks and dangers. What would be a minor inconvenience on I–80, like a flat tire, can be a nasty affair indeed in the backcountry if you are not properly prepared. You won't be able to call AAA, and you can't count on someone else driving by anytime soon. These are not country lanes, but rudimentary mountain roads. With the proper precautions, however, the risks inherent in backcountry motoring can be minimized.

This book is not intended for serious off–roaders, although the beauty of the places it describes should appeal to all. No winches, oversize tires or lift kits are needed. On most of the trips, four-wheel drive is needed occasionally, not constantly, but I assume you'll have it when you need it. I also assume you'll take these drives when weather and road conditions in the mountains are best, usually about mid–July through mid–October. But road conditions can and do change in the backcountry. I've found my way blocked by snowbanks as late as mid–August.

Most of the time all you'll need to bring along are some basic supplies, a sense of adventure, a desire to explore, and a craving to witness the startling grandeur of two of the highest ranges in the United States, the Sierra Nevada Mountains and their neighboring range to the east, the dry and sparsely vegetated White Mountains. You'll also visit a third range, the Sweetwater Mountains, also east of the Sierras.

Some of the drives are easy cruises. Others have moments that will seem difficult as you approach them, but easy once you've gotten through. A few, like Silver Canyon in the White Mountains, are hair–raising because of the steep mountainside routes they follow. On just about all the drives you'll come across side roads that are not described. That's because there are so many of these spurs, which usually are rougher than the main trails, that it would be impractical to take and describe them all. So I've focused mostly on main routes, but you certainly can do some exploring on your own.

My primary goal is to help you experience the Sierra Nevada region in a unique way. But I also want you to gain an appreciation of the region's fragile environment, which I hope you'll protect as well as enjoy. Along with some of the most unspoiled scenery in the state, you'll get glimpses of what logging, mining, development and greed have done to our public lands and waterways. So the drives should educate while you recreate.

The trips will help you sense the state's culture and history as well as its natural environment. Some of the roads are old mining routes that will take you to ghost towns and other relics of California's past.

Each trip includes the location, the U.S. Forest Service map you'll need, estimated time and distance, a description, and some of the interesting sights along the way. They also include places to stop so the kids can romp, chomp down on a burger or tour a museum.

All of the drives will astound you with this central realization: Even in such a crowded state, with a sport–utility vehicle it is quite easy to go in a few hours from congested freeways and smoggy cities to places of solitude, peace, beauty and adventure.

For millions of Americans, the switch from sedans and station wagons to sport-utility vehicles has been a way to show that we're not really tamed city slickers and suburbanites, at least not at heart. The decision to buy a family-style four-wheeler helps keep the explorer in us alive.

I hope this book does the same.

Tony Huegel

Making it fun for all

The lump on the head that my daughter brought home from her first backcountry tour disappeared years ago. Not so the memory of that baptism by bumps.

She was three then. Our family car — a comfortable four–wheel drive sport–utility vehicle complete with stereo and air conditioning — was shiny and new. We were yuppies, and we felt inadmissible at any price to the league of serious four-wheelers who descend on Moab, Utah, each April.

Jungle Jim I was not. Jungle James, maybe.

The windows were up. The air was on. We probably had some James Taylor tape plugged in as the intricately carved red canyons rolled by, but I don't recall.

And there in the back seat was Hannah, strapped securely to her personal cassette player and plugged snugly into her car seat. Tom Glazer, who makes charming recordings for children, crooned on about his nose and toes. Coloring pens in hand, paper propped up, Hannah was ready for the rocks.

But not the rolls.

Off we went through one of the best backcountry driving areas in North America, Canyonlands National Park.

Suddenly the vehicle pitched from one side to the other as we went over a bump. Instantly we heard the kind of sound no one wants to hear so far from Mr. Goodwrench.

Slam!

Heavy metal against sedimentary rock? No. It was the sound of Hannah's head making solid contact with the window beside her.

The window was unscathed. Her head, she announced, was not, at least not by her diagnosis. And as the day went on she complained to no end about what the road's uneven quality was doing to her efforts to color within the lines. But there was no harm done that a picnic and plenty of rest stops didn't cure.

That was years ago. She has more typical adolescent activities keeping her busy now. And my wife, Lynn, a Connecticut–bred school teacher, often has other demands on her time, like the never–ending search for reasons to not grade the essay tests she gave three weeks ago. So much of the time my buddy in the backcountry is my son, Land, who is four now. To him, transit involves two distinct categories: gway woads (paved), and bumpy woads (dirt).

Trying to keep kids, especially teenagers, happy on car trips has always been tough. But there are many things you can do to make touring the backcountry as fun and interesting for them as it is for you.

Probably the best general advice I can give is this: Don't just drive. Stop, and stop often.

Children love water, unless it's in a tub. Bring rain boots or sandals, and let them play for a few minutes now and then at the little streams and ponds you'll see along the way. Pick up a gold pan at a souvenir store and do a little streamside panning. Trips that include ghost towns or old cabins and such will be big hits.

Bring a magnifying glass. Inspect, touch and smell the wildflowers, the insects, the different types of rocks and trees. There's nothing like running a hand over the exposed wood of a western bristlecone pine that is thousands of years old, or across the bark of a towering Jeffrey pine. Get some good books on identifying wildflowers, birds, insects, rocks, trees and animals in the region. Get books on the geology and history of the area. They're available at Forest Service offices, local bookstores and visitors centers.

Make a photocopy of the area on the map where you'll be going. Get each child an inexpensive compass. Let them help you navigate and identify peaks, creeks, mine sites and other landmarks.

Let each child pack his or her favorite books and toys, but don't cram the car with stuff.

Bring at least one personal cassette player. Before leaving, go to your local public library and check out some cassette tapes for children. Better yet, buy some. You'll make good use of them for years to come.

Some of my children's favorites over the years have included recordings by Tom Glazer, Raffi and the Sesame Street bunch. The Wee Sing series has also helped keep the peace.

Books on tape, something I listen to myself on long highway drives, are great diversions for children, too. Some video rental stores carry them.

Other items that have bought us quiet and good humor in the back seat are an inexpensive point–and–shoot camera the kids can use, and toy binoculars. Now and then my son likes to have a notebook and pencil so he can pretend he's taking notes about our journeys just like dad.

If you have a responsible, licensed teenage driver on board, let him or her drive the safer and easier stretches. The sooner they learn backcountry driving skills, the longer they'll remain eager participants.

Of course, you must bring snacks, preferably the nutritious, non–sticky kind, and drinks. Be sure cups have secure tops that you can poke straws through. Plastic garbage bags, paper towels, changes of clothing (particularly socks) and wet wipes are good to have along, too.

Plan a picnic. See the sights. Hike to some hilltop. Cast a line. Bring your mountain bikes. And don't forget pillows for the sleepy. Finally, do something nice when the drive is over: Go out to dinner.

Whether you travel with children or not, don't make the drive everything. Make it part of a day that takes in the huge range of experiences that make the Sierra Nevada Mountains so special.

Rules of the road

One of the best things about life in the West is the vast amount of public land, land owned by you and me. Much of that land has been explored and used by miners, loggers and ranchers off and on for more than a century. The result: roads all over the place, not just the nicely graded sort, but the adventurous kind you may have been thinking of when you bought your 4x4.

These roads can vary from well-maintained gravel to rough and rocky two-track trails. The goal of this book is to help you find some of the most driveable, scenic and interesting routes. I want you to enjoy safe travel off the beaten path without losing the sense of adventure and discovery.

Here are some tips that will help:

KNOW WHERE YOU'RE GOING. The maps in this book are not intended for navigation. They are only at–a–glance maps to give you a general idea of where the drives are. I recommend U.S. Forest Service maps. They're good all–round maps, although they don't show elevation contours as topographic maps do. In some cases they do misrepresent the quality of a road, and sometimes the maps for adjoining national forests or districts are not consistent in how they depict the same roads. Nor do they show all the roads in an area. But they're cheap. You can buy them along the way at district offices, visitors centers and local map retailers. For this book you'll need six national forest maps: Eldorado, Stanislaus, Inyo, Tahoe and Toiyabe (both Bridgeport and Carson City ranger districts). You might also pick up a copy of each forest's travel map. They show which roads are open or closed to which uses. But they can be difficult to read and understand. Outdoor equipment stores carry U.S. Geological Survey topographic maps that show elevations and more detail than the Forest Service maps. You might have to buy more than one for each trip, so they can become pricey. But they are the best, in my view. Carefully study your maps before you leave. And do bring them with you.

BE CAREFUL. Don't take chances. Don't be tempted by excessively steep, rocky stretches or muddy bogs. Know your vehicle. Don't over-estimate what it can do. Many 4x4 owners will testify that they never got stuck so often or so badly before they bought a vehicle they thought could go anywhere. Always remember that help can be a long way off. Wear your seat belt, and have children in proper safety restraints. Always check the weather forecast before setting out, and watch for changes.

Guidebooks dealing with public lands advise readers to check with the appropriate land management agency, usually the U.S. Forest Service or Bureau of Land Management, for the latest road conditions. That's good advice. But the most knowledgeable people are often in the field and unavailable, I've found. In my experience, asking for the latest conditions hasn't always worked.

BE PREPARED. Here's a checklist of some things to have:
❏ A good first aid kit, with plenty of ointment and bandages for the inevitable scraped knees and elbows.
❏ Fire permit, free at any Forest Service office.

❏ Very good tires, a good spare and jack, tire sealant, an air pump, and a small board to support the jack on dirt; a full gas tank.

❏ Food and drinks. Some places, like the White Mountains, have no water, so bring plenty. I carry a water filter, too, just in case I need to draw water from a stream.

❏ Supplies, like sleeping bags and warm clothing, for spending the night in case you must.

❏ In case you run into trouble, bring some basic tools, including jumper cables, duct tape, baling wire, spare fuses, Swiss Army knife, folding saw, high–strength tow strap, small folding shovel and a plastic sheet to put on the ground. An assortment of screws, washers and nuts could come in handy, too.

❏ Maps; compass
❏ Extra eyeglasses and car keys
❏ Camera (still or video), film or video tape, tripod, binoculars
❏ Litter bag
❏ Flashlight or head lamp, extra batteries
❏ Matches
❏ Roadside emergency reflectors
❏ Altimeter, just for fun
❏ Watch
❏ Hats, jackets and other clothing suitable for possible adverse weather
❏ Insect repellent
❏ Toilet paper, paper towels

I keep much of this stuff ready to go in one of those large plastic carry–all containers you can buy just about anywhere. I'm often out alone scouting new drives, so I bring my mountain bike in case I get into a serious bind. I also use it to scout places that might damage my vehicle. If you do a lot of this stuff, think about getting a CB radio, even though their range is limited. Someday, when there are enough satellites or whatever up in space, I'm going to get a cellular telephone.

I also have some tips on what to wear.

Forget shorts. Shorts are dumb. Why would anyone expose his or her legs to brush, rocks, bugs and burning high–elevation sun? Loose cotton pants and a loose cotton shirt, with breast pockets and sleeves you can roll up or down as needed, are best. I also recommend high–topped leather boots with lug soles. If you're like me, you're going to do a lot of scrambling around to get that perfect camera angle. Ankle–high boots let too much debris in.

KNOW THE RULES. There are some, even in places where it's likely no one will be looking. The intent behind them is to keep you safe. They also help to preserve these places from the kind of abuse and destruction that disturbs wildlife, interferes with other lawful uses like livestock grazing, or causes environmental damage. Misconduct and mistakes can result in personal injury, damage to your vehicle and areas being closed.

So please ...

• Leave a friend or relative with a copy of your map showing the routes you plan to take. Let the person know when you'll return, and whom to call if you don't. There's nothing like having a spare vehicle just in case, so invite a friend to come along in his or her vehicle, too.

• Camp only in established campsites, whether developed or primitive.

• Don't disturb wildlife or livestock. Keep your distance.

• Take out only what you bring in. Clean up after yourself and others. Don't remove any archaeological or historic artifacts. Be extremely careful around old mining operations. They're very dangerous, especially for children. View them from a distance.

• Avoid parking on grass; hot exhaust systems can ignite fires. Avoid steep hillsides, stream banks and meadows.

• If you get stuck or lost, stay with your vehicle. It'll be easier to find than you will be if you're walking through the mountains. Your vehicle will provide shelter, too.

• Finally, remember that the miners and loggers who carved these roads into the mountains over the last century didn't have the latest highway safety regulations in mind. Spurs from the main roads can be very rough. If the going does gets real rough, and it shouldn't on the drives in this book, ask yourself if it's worth the risk to you, your passengers and your vehicle. Believe me, it's not.

You might also contact or join Tread Lightly!, Inc., an organization founded to promote environmentally responsible use of off–highway vehicles. It is based in Ogden, Utah. Call 1–800–966–9900.

DRIVE SMART. There are some driving techniques that can help you get where you're going and back again, safely.

• Drive responsibly. Never drive in designated wilderness areas, which are usually marked with signs. Go only where motorized vehicles are permitted. Stay on the established road. Never make a new trail. Obey regulatory and private property signs. Try not to spin your tires, which digs up the ground. Cross streams only at established crossings. Close gates behind you.

• Consider the time of day before you set out. Is it getting late? Don't get caught out there in the dark.

• Learn how to work your four–wheel drive system before setting out. Think ahead as you drive; engage 4wd before you need it, not when you need it. When in doubt, scout. Walk uncertain stretches of trail before you drive them.

• Use your low–range gears, which can make braking and clutching unnecessary, to climb or descend steep hills and to inch through the inevitable tight spots without stalling. Avoid traversing steep hillsides. Even if the road goes that way, use good judgment and turn back if you're not confident it's safe. Don't try to turn around on a steep hillside. Back out. When climbing a steep hill, or going through mud, snow or sand, don't stop midway. Doing so could mean lost traction and stalling. Momentum can be everything, so keep moving. If you do stall going up a hill and must get out of the vehicle, put it in low–range first gear or reverse, and set the parking brake. Solidly block the wheels. When you try to get going again, play the parking brake against the clutch so you don't roll backwards. If you must back down a steep hill, put your vehicle in low–range reverse for slow, easy control, and stay off the gas pedal. Also use your low–range gears to steadily ease yourself down steep, loose terrain. Remember that vehicles driving uphill have the right of way, because it's easier and safer for the vehicle going downhill to stop and back up the hill.

• Have a passenger or another driver guide you through difficult spots. If the road has deep ruts, straddle them, letting them pass beneath the vehicle while the wheels ride high on the sides. Check your vehicle's clearance before driving over obstacles. Don't let rocks and such hit the big round parts, sometimes called "pumpkins," of your front and rear axles. Cracking or punching a hole in one will let vital oil drain out and expose the gears to dust and dirt. If I can't go around such a rock, I let it pass slowly almost beneath my seat or the passenger seat, where there's greater clearance. Or run a tire over the obstacle. Cross obstacles at an angle.

• Inspect streams closely before crossing. Cross slowly.

• Many times you'll find that your low–range gears will provide both greater control and the high revs you need at slow speeds. I use mine a lot. If your engine bogs down often in high range, switch to low range.

• If you must cross soft material such as sand or mud, lower your vehicle's tire pressure to 15 to 20 pounds. That provides a wider footprint and greater flotation. The problem is that if a service station is far off, you'll need either a hand pump or a small electric air compressor, like those available at department stores, to get your tires back up to proper inflation when you return to pavement. Again, momentum can mean everything; keep the vehicle moving.

• If you get stuck, calmly analyze the situation. With thought and work, you'll probably get out. Don't spin your tires if you get bogged down. That'll dig you in deeper. Use the folding shovel you packed to dig out around the tires, and jam rocks, branches, sticks and such around the tires for traction. If you get high–centered, meaning your undercarriage is lodged on something high and your tires have daylight between them and the ground, take out your jack and the little board you brought to set it on. Carefully jack up the vehicle, little by little, placing rocks, dirt and other materials under each tire to build a base for it to rest on.

• When going through rocks or rutted stretches, keep your hands loose on the steering wheel, at 10 and 2 o'clock. Keep your thumbs on top of the wheel. If a front tire hits a rock or rut, the steering wheel could be jerked in an unexpected direction, injuring a thumb with a steering wheel spoke.

READ. You'll enjoy your ventures into the Sierra Nevada much more if you know something about the amazing geology, flora, fauna and history of the region. Do some reading. Bookstores, visitors centers and other places have many fine titles to choose from. I highly recommend Sue Irwin's *California's Eastern Sierra; A Visitor's Guide*, published by Cachuma Press in cooperation with the Eastern Sierra Interpretive Association. It's a beautifully illustrated all–round guide to the region. For a good geologic read, pick up a copy of Mary Hill's *Geology of the Sierra Nevada*, published by University of California Press. It not only describes geologic features, but tells you where you can go to see them. The Yosemite Association and the Sequoia Natural History Association, in cooperation with the National Park Service, publish a series of books on Sierra Nevada trees, birds, mammals, reptiles and amphibians under the *"Discovering"* theme. Water is everything in the dry American West. To understand what that has meant to human settlement and development of the West, especially the Owens Valley and Mono Basin, read Marc Reisner's riveting book, *Cadillac Desert: The American West and Its Disappearing Water*, published by Penguin Books.

HAVE FUN! You can easily justify the expense of a sport-utility vehicle, especially in a state with so much beautiful public land. As you travel the backcountry, tell me what you've found, whether it's mistakes in the book or additional trips and tips you'd like to see added in future editions.

You and your SUV

Modern sport–utility vehicles — Jeep Cherokees, Ford Explorers, Toyota 4Runners, Chevrolet Blazers and such — are built to take families places that sedans, vans and station wagons either cannot go, or shouldn't. Despite their comforts, they are rugged transport. Equipped with four–wheel drive, protective steel skid plates, high ground clearance and all–terrain tires, they can go from the showroom straight into the hills without modifications. But backcountry roads can give even the toughest SUV quite a workout.

So if you're the type who likes to leave the pavement, you've got to give your SUV more attention than you might be accustomed to giving a car.

Start with your owner's manual. (It's in the glove compartment, right?) You may see two maintenance categories designed for two basic driving conditions: severe, and everything else.

Anyone who owns this book falls into the severe category, and must do more maintenance.

For example:

❏ Instead of changing your oil — a remarkably cheap and effective way to prolong engine life — at 7,500 miles, change it no later than every 3,000 miles or even sooner if you do a lot of driving on dirt roads. I use synthetic engine oil. It costs three or four times more than regular oil, but my opinion is that the superior protection is worth a few more dollars. With a vehicle that costs as much as many people earn in a year, I'm not about to skimp on my engine's lifeblood. Besides, I get many more miles out of what's in my oil pan than what's in my gas tank.

❏ Instead of getting a lube job at 15,000 miles, get one no later than every 7,500 miles.

❏ Inspect your air filter at least every 3,000 miles. It's cheap and easy to replace, so don't skimp there, either.

❏ Don't neglect gearbox oils, wheel bearing grease and coolant. Follow your owner's manual.

❏ Check the tires. No part of your SUV will take a greater beating than your tires. Inspect them, including your spare, closely before, during and after your drive. Sierra granite is punishing stuff. Do not rely on all–season highway tires. Along with heavy–duty shock absorbers designed for off–highway use, I recommend all–terrain tires.

❏ When you get home, head for the car wash. Thoroughly clean the vehicle. Put extra effort into the undercarriage, particularly the wheel wells, because dirt harbors moisture, and moisture feeds the beast that never sleeps: rust.

In short, maintain your SUV exceptionally well. In the backcountry, a reliable vehicle is your family's best friend.

Trail descriptions

Saying a backcountry drive is fun, easy, hard, rough, long or short can be quite subjective. Much of that interpretation depends on the individual's experience, likes and dislikes, perceptions and circumstances. I've tried to bring some objectivity to the various categories I've used to describe each drive, but that can only go so far. Anyway, here's what's behind each category:

LOCATION: Where the drive is. The drives are arranged from north to south.

HIGHLIGHTS: What's best about the drive.

DIFFICULTY: This is subjective. I've assumed you are not a hard–core four–wheeler, but just somebody in a modern sport–utility vehicle who's looking for some reasonably safe adventure. The ratings are: *easy*, which means it's a real cruise that won't require four–wheel drive; *moderate*, which means you will need four–wheel drive at least now and then, the going will be slow, and you can expect occasional rough spots; and *difficult*, which means rough and slow, using four–wheel drive most of the time, and a higher likelihood that you'll scrape your undercarriage's protective skid plates on rocks. The latter moments are few in this book.

TIME & DISTANCE: The estimated time it takes to complete the drive, excluding your travel time getting to the starting point. The time element can vary enormously for each drive, depending on how much time you want to spend at stops along the way. Since odometer accuracy varies among vehicles, your measurements of distances might differ somewhat from mine. But they shouldn't differ much.

GETTING THERE: This will direct you to the starting point.

THE DRIVE: Details of the trip, such as what turns to take, where you'll end up, how far it is from here to there, and what you'll see along the way.

REST STOPS: Where you can stop for a picnic, to camp, buy a bite to eat, explore a ghost town, visit a museum, etc.

GETTING HOME: This will vary according to where home is. But there are usually common exit points leading to highways.

MAP: Each trip recommends a specific U.S. Forest Service map that you can buy at one of their district offices, and at visitors centers and map retailers. They are good all–round maps and information resources. But there are other maps you can buy. U.S. Geological Survey maps, available at outdoor equipment stores, are excellent.

INFORMATION: A telephone number you can call for road conditions or other information. The book also contains a separate listing of Forest Service and other addresses relevant to exploring the Sierra Nevada Mountains.

Author's favorites

I'm picky.

I like grand vistas, high peaks, broad plateaus, lush meadows, sparkling lakes and high elevations. I like to feel close to the top of the world, and as though there's no one else around. I like to see geologic forces at work. I like variety, and the illusion that I'm exploring far from civilization.

Those are the values that guided me in deciding which of the drives in this book are my favorites. But believe me, the choices didn't come easily.

BOWMAN LAKE LOOP: The terrain varies from canyons to forest, valleys and serene lakes. It includes the site of an old gold town, Summit City, complete with cemetery.

THE LAKE TAHOE VISTAS: Mt. Watson, Martis Peak and Genoa Peak offer unsurpassed, panoramic views of the Tahoe Basin and beyond. And after each drive, you get to return to all those lakeside hot spots.

DUNDERBERG MEADOW ROAD: Aspen groves in autumn, views that go from the Mono Basin and Nevada's ranges to the high Sierra, the side trip to the high unnamed lake, and the fact that this is one of the most relaxing backcountry cruises you'll find anywhere give this drive special appeal.

WHITE MOUNTAINS LOOP: I've never been to the Peruvian altiplano, but the high, rolling crest of these dry mountains — the second–highest in California after the Sierra Nevada Mountains — is how I've always imagined it. They are the highest range in the Great Basin, and the inhospitable home to the world's oldest living organisms, the rare western bristlecone pines. Plus, you get great views of the Sierra Nevada, to the west across the Owens Valley. The steep drive up or down Silver Canyon is exhilarating, even a bit scary. It's probably not a good route for people who are new to mountain driving.

COYOTE FLAT: As you gain and lose thousands of feet in elevation, this drive offers an amazing transition from the desert floor of the Owens Valley to high, sub–alpine meadows, glacial moraines, and views of Sierra glaciers, including Palisade Glacier, the largest glacier still in existence in the Sierra Nevada and the southernmost active glacier in the United States. The return trip, if taken in late afternoon when shadows are cast and the light is richer in color, is astoundingly beautiful and geologically fascinating.

Map symbols

Points of interest	▭	Forest Service road	03
Paved road	∿	Interstate highway	80
Easy dirt road	∿	State highway	50
Primitive road	∿	State road	89
Campground	▲		
Lakes	◗	North indicator	N
Streams	∿		
Mountain	⛰		
Ranger station	⚑		
Picnic area	⊼		
City or town	○		

Trips indicated in color

Paved road	
Easy dirt road	
Primitive road	∿

Guide for trip activities

Canoeing	Swimming	Historic sites	Fishing	Photo opportunities

Restaurant	Hiking	Biking	Picnicking	Camping

THE
DRIVES

The grave of Summit City founder H.W. Hartley, on the Bowman Lake Loop.

The site of Summit City, a short-lived boom town.

Grouse Ridge Road

LOCATION: Nevada County north of Yuba Pass on Interstate 80 & U.S. 20.

HIGHLIGHTS: Road ends in a campground in an area with many pretty lakes and basins. Great hiking and mountain biking. Sweeping vista from an old fire lookout. A gem.

DIFFICULTY: Easy.

TIME & DISTANCE: About 2 hours and 27 miles round–trip from I–80. I recommend it as a weekend camping trip.

GETTING THERE: About 3.7 miles west of where U.S. 20 and I–80 intersect at Yuba Pass, turn north from U.S. 20 toward Bowman Lake on Forest Road 18. Set the odometer at 0.

THE DRIVE: From U.S. 20, FR 18, a narrow paved road, winds through forest for 1.4 miles and crosses a creek. The road then winds up a canyon with some very nice views. At 6.3 miles turn right onto FR 14, the Grouse Ridge Road. You're at about 5,600 feet now, and you'll climb higher. By 9.2 miles you'll get some nice Sierra Nevada vistas to the left as you emerge from the trees into an open area. The road now becomes considerably rougher, but still easy. After another 1.5 miles you'll round a turn and see beautiful Grouse Lakes Basin, the kind of place many people backpack in to see elsewhere in the Sierras. As you enter the campground above the basin there's a short hiking trail to the right, to a knoll with a great view. From the parking area at the far end of the campground you can hike a short distance to the old lookout tower for a stunning, top o' the world view from 7,707 feet.

REST STOPS: The Grouse Ridge Campground is a lovely place, quiet but for California's ever–present jets and airplanes. It has toilets, tables, etc.

GETTING HOME: U.S. 20 or I–80 east and west.

MAP: Tahoe National Forest.

INFORMATION: Nevada City District, (916) 265–4531.

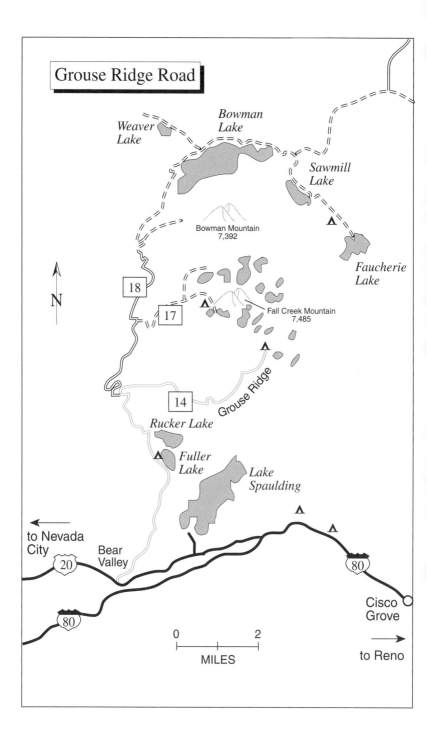

Grouse Ridge Road

Weaver Lake

Bowman Lake

Sawmill Lake

Bowman Mountain 7,392

Faucherie Lake

N

18

17

Fall Creek Mountain 7,485

14

Grouse Ridge

Rucker Lake

Fuller Lake

Lake Spaulding

to Nevada City

20

Bear Valley

80

80

Cisco Grove

to Reno

0   2
MILES

Bowman Lake Loop

TRIP 2

LOCATION: Nevada County, north of Yuba Pass on Interstate 80 and U.S. 20.

HIGHLIGHTS: Canyons, lakes, old town site and cemetery.

DIFFICULTY: Easy.

TIME & DISTANCE: 2 days. But there's so much to see and do that I recommend it for a 3–day weekend, so bring your camping gear. About 90 miles with optional side trips. Bring water, and a filter for getting more.

GETTING THERE: About 3.7 miles west of where U.S. 20 and I–80 intersect at Yuba Pass, turn north from U.S. 20 toward Bowman Lake on Forest Road 18, west of Lake Spaulding.

THE DRIVE: It winds through the northern Sierras' lake country. At the Grouse Ridge turnoff, go straight toward Bowman Lake, about 14 forested miles north of U.S. 20. The first 10.2 miles are paved, then it becomes a rough but easy mountain road. Take the side trip to Carr and Feeley lakes. Weaver Lake, about 1.2 miles northwest of Bowman Lake, is a pretty place to camp and canoe. Go east along Bowman Lake. From Jackson Creek Campground, it's 1.1 miles to beautiful Sawmill Lake. About 3 miles farther, past some decent camp-sites, is the Faucherie Lake Recreation Area. Fine boating. From Jackson Creek Campground, it's 6 miles to Jackson Meadow. You can cut the drive short by going that way and taking the paved road to I–80. Or you can continue southward past gorgeous Catfish Lake for about 6.5 scenic miles to the site of once–bustling Summit City (check out the graveyard) and Meadow Lake. Summit City, founded in 1862 by H.W. Hartley, had 5,000 people in 1864. But the gold that caused the boom proved too difficult to extract, and the city soon died. Hartley's resting place is well–marked in the cemetery. Head toward Webber Lake, 9 miles, and Highway 89, 16 miles away. About 3 miles from Meadow Lake is the 10–mile round–trip spur to White Rock Lake, which is nice but buggy and perhaps not worthwhile if time is limited. If you take it, watch for directions painted on trees.

REST STOPS: Good but primitive camping at Weaver Lake and at Catfish Lake. Or try Jackson Creek Campground.

GETTING HOME: From Webber Lake, go east and then south to Truckee and I–80.

MAP: Tahoe National Forest.

INFORMATION: Nevada City Ranger District, (916) 265–4531; Sierraville Ranger District, (916) 994–3401.

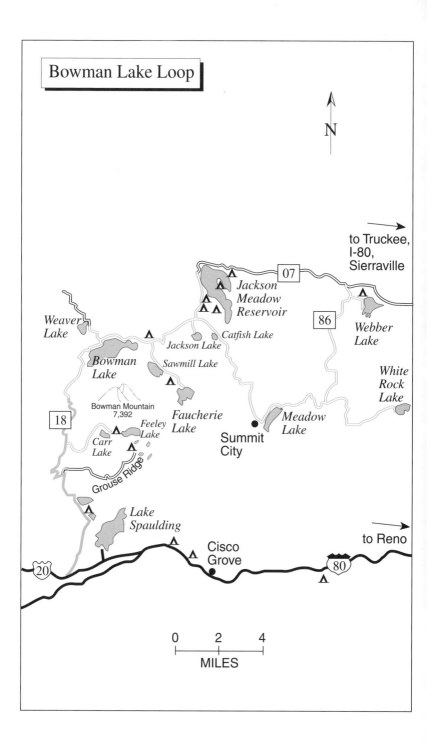

Bowman Lake Loop

N

to Truckee,
I-80,
Sierraville

07

86

Jackson
Meadow
Reservoir

Webber
Lake

Weaver
Lake

Catfish Lake

Jackson Lake

White
Rock
Lake

Bowman
Lake

Sawmill Lake

Bowman Mountain
7,392

Faucherie
Lake

Feeley
Lake

Meadow
Lake

18

Carr
Lake

Summit
City

Grouse Ridge

Lake
Spaulding

to Reno

Cisco
Grove

20

80

| 0 | 2 | 4 |

MILES

Crystal Peak Loop

LOCATION: Overlooks Dog Valley, just west of the California/Nevada line about 5 miles straight northwest of Verdi, Nev., which is 10 miles west of Reno on Interstate 80.

HIGHLIGHTS: Sweeping views of Nevada's mountain ranges, Reno and Dog Valley.

DIFFICULTY: Easy.

TIME & DISTANCE: An hour, 7.5 miles.

GETTING THERE: From Verdi take the Dog Valley Road, a.k.a. Bridge Street, northwest about 6.25 miles to Dog Valley Campground, which is not particularly appealing. The drive, on Forest Road 038, starts here.

THE DRIVE: You'll be driving through an area where crystal for radios was mined during World War II. Go 1.5 miles or so from the campground to an unsigned fork. Go left, taking in the views to the southeast. Soon you'll pass through some narrow brush (snap off the branches that'll do a job on your paint). You'll come to another fork, where you'll go straight. You'll quickly see some magnificent views. You can see 8,089-foot Crystal Peak up ahead as you drive along the side of the mountain. Pass through a small gully. You'll drive on a road of granulated crystal, and then start descending from about 7,200 feet to about 6,200 feet at the campground.

REST STOPS: Lovely Crystal Peak Park along the Truckee River at the west end of Verdi. I stop there whenever I'm passing through on I–80.

GETTING HOME: I–80 east or west.

MAP: Toiyabe National Forest, Carson Ranger District.

INFORMATION: Carson District, (702) 882–2766.

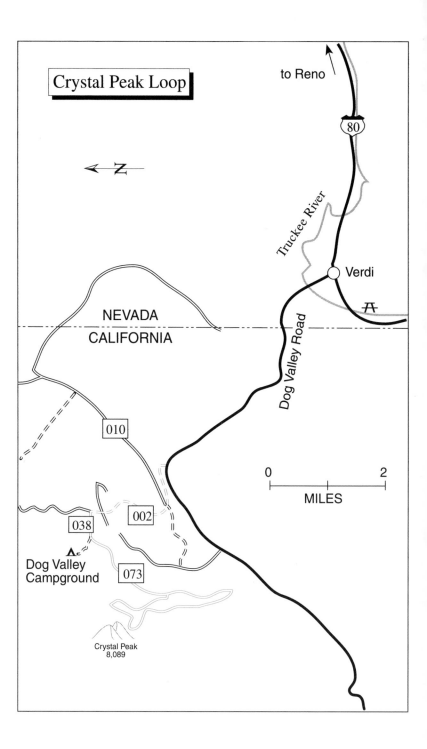

Crystal Peak Loop

to Reno

80

Truckee River

Verdi

NEVADA

CALIFORNIA

Dog Valley Road

010

0   2
MILES

002

038

073

Dog Valley
Campground

Crystal Peak
8,089

Martis Peak Vista

LOCATION: Almost 4 miles due north of Kings Beach at Lake Tahoe's north end.

HIGHLIGHTS: Stunning views of the Tahoe Basin and surrounding region, including Donner Lake, from an old fire lookout atop Martis Peak (8,656 ft.).

DIFFICULTY: Easy to moderate. Steep and a bit rocky toward the end.

TIME & DISTANCE: About 1.5 hours or less and 8 miles round–trip from state Highway 267. This is not a loop.

GETTING THERE: Drive about 3.2 miles northwest from Kings Beach, or about 8 miles southeast from Truckee, on Highway 267 toward Brockway Summit (7,199 ft.). A short distance north of the summit, take the first eastbound road, Forest Road 1802, up Martis Creek. Set your odometer to 0.

THE DRIVE: After turning up Martis Creek, drive 1.9 miles, passing through a logging area, to an intersection. Take FR 1692 up ahead. You might see something like "Martis Pk" spray painted on a tree trunk to indicate the way. At 2.6 miles you'll come to another intersection. Go straight. You'll be driving on dusty logging roads of loose soil. At almost 3.3 miles you'll come to a fork. A rough trail, FR 92B, goes straight, and you don't want that. Go left on the unsigned fork. About a half–mile farther the road will become steep and rocky. You might want to use low range. Vistas will appear, and soon you'll see the old fire lookout. Drive up to it and park. You're at 8,656 feet now. (Lake Tahoe, down below, is at 6,229 ft.) Climb up the fire lookout and take in an amazing sight.

REST STOPS: The summit.

GETTING HOME: Highway 267 north to Truckee or south to Kings Beach and Lake Tahoe.

MAP: Tahoe National Forest.

INFORMATION: U.S. Forest Service's Lake Tahoe Basin Management Unit, (916) 573–2600; Lake Tahoe Visitors Center, (916) 573–2674.

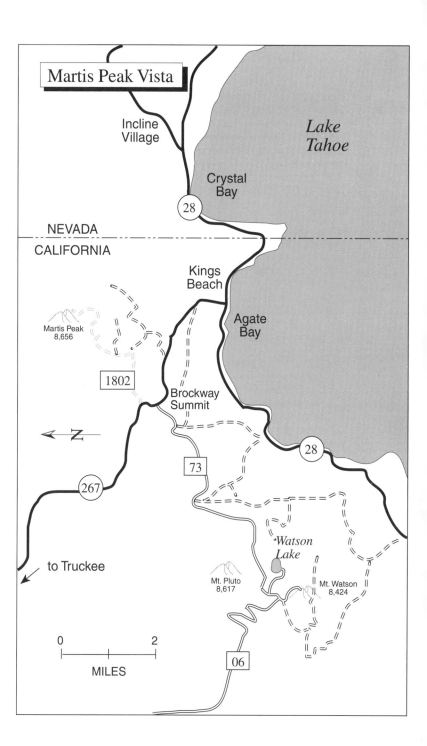

Martis Peak Vista

Incline Village

Lake Tahoe

Crystal Bay

28

NEVADA
CALIFORNIA

Kings Beach

Agate Bay

Martis Peak
8,656

1802

Brockway
Summit

N

73

28

267

to Truckee

Watson Lake

Mt. Pluto
8,617

Mt. Watson
8,424

0   2
MILES

06

Mt. Watson Tahoe Vista

LOCATION: Placer County, about 3 miles due west of Lake Tahoe's north end.

HIGHLIGHTS: Grand view of the Tahoe Basin from the top of 8,424–foot Mt. Watson. More great views of the Sierras on the way down.

DIFFICULTY: Easy to moderate. This is not a loop.

TIME & DISTANCE: About 1.5 hours and 18 miles round–trip with the spur to Watson Lake. Longer if you picnic at the summit, take photos, yodel.

GETTING THERE: From Kings Beach at Lake Tahoe's north end, go northwest on state Highway 267 about 3.2 miles to Brockway Summit (7,199 ft.). At the summit turn left (west) onto Mt. Watson Road, a.k.a. Forest Road 73. From Truckee, it's a little more than 8 miles south on Highway 267 to Brockway Summit.

THE DRIVE: Set your odometer to 0 immediately upon turning onto the Mt. Watson Road. For the first 4 miles you'll be on a good gravel road as you drive through the forest. Then the gravel quits, and the roadbed becomes cobble–like. At about 5.9 miles you'll come to FR 16N73C on the left. It goes about 0.7 miles to Watson Lake. It's a little rough, but easy. From this turnoff, it's about 0.7 miles to FR 73M, a moderate two–track that branches sharply to the left from the main road. It's about 1.6 miles to the summit along a mountainside. You might want to use low range going up for better control. The view from the summit is absolutely magnificent. There's a great photo opportunity on the rock outcrop you'll see. You did bring camera and film, right? It's great going down, too, but of course the driver will miss it *because he or she is paying close attention to the road.*

REST STOPS: There's camping and picnicking at Watson Lake, but this is such a short drive that I recommend lunch at the summit. You might also stop at Sugar Pine Point State Park on the lake's west side.

GETTING HOME: Go back to Highway 267. From there it's north to Truckee or south to Kings Beach.

MAP: Tahoe National Forest.

INFORMATION: U.S. Forest Service's Lake Tahoe Basin Management Unit, (916) 573–2600; Lake Tahoe Visitors Center, (916) 573–2674.

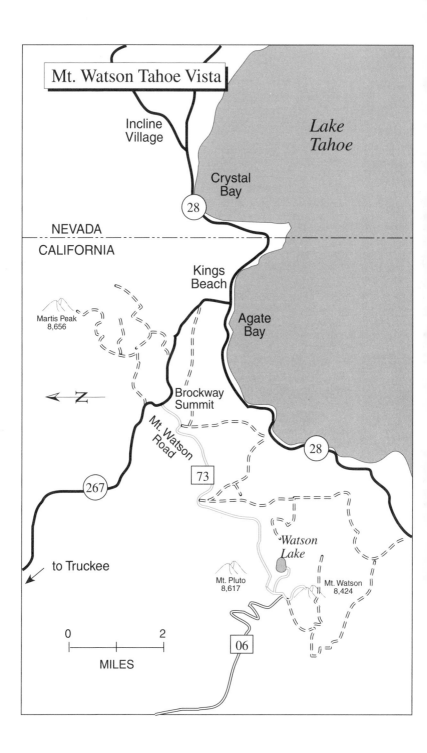

Mt. Watson Tahoe Vista

Incline Village

Lake Tahoe

Crystal Bay

28

NEVADA

CALIFORNIA

Kings Beach

Agate Bay

Martis Peak
8,656

← N

Brockway Summit

Mt. Watson Road

28

267

73

to Truckee

Watson Lake

Mt. Pluto
8,617

Mt. Watson
8,424

0 — 2
MILES

06

Barker Pass Loop

LOCATION: West of Lake Tahoe's McKinney Bay.

HIGHLIGHTS: Lakes, waterfowl, mountain vistas.

DIFFICULTY: The first 6.5 miles or so are rough. I'll rate that leg moderate. Then it improves to an easy rating.

TIME & DISTANCE: About an hour and 4.8 miles from Tahoma to pretty Miller Lake. Entire loop is about 30 miles and at least 3 hours. Add an hour or so if you explore spurs, picnic, etc.

GETTING THERE: Turn southwest off Highway 89 at Tahoma onto McKinney–Rubicon Springs Road. A quarter–mile later, go left at the fork, following the sign on the tree. Continue following the signs to a stop sign. Go straight across the road. You'll see a sign saying Miller Lake, 4 miles. There's an off–highway vehicle staging area a short distance farther. Set your odometer to 0 there.

THE DRIVE: The road immediately gets rough. Along the way you may see some serious off–roaders heading to or returning from the notorious Rubicon Trail. (Forget it.) By 2.3 miles you'll pass lily–covered McKinney Lake on the left, and then Lily Lake. Soon you'll come to Miller Lake, which has nice campsites (no facilities), geese and ducks to keep the kids entertained. There's more solitude at Richardson Lake, which is an easy mile up a left turn just beyond Miller Lake. About 1.2 miles from Miller Lake you'll pass the Rubicon turnoff. At 6.4 miles there's a fork. Keep to the left. Soon you'll see pretty Bear Lake below on the left. About 2.7 miles from the Bear Lake turnoff is a narrow two–track to the right that climbs 1.8 miles to Barker Pass. If it's dry, it's a pretty but narrow alternative to the main road. If you stay on the main road, about 5 miles from Bear Lake you'll come to a T intersection. Go right for some neat views on the way to Barker Pass. It's about a half–mile from the summit to pavement and another 6.9 miles to the highway.

REST STOPS: Miller and Bear lakes for camping, canoeing. Lots of waterfowl to watch at Miller Lake. Try nearby Sugar Pine Point State Park.

GETTING HOME: North or south on Highway 89.

MAP: Tahoe National Forest.

INFORMATION: Lake Tahoe Basin Management Unit, (916) 573–2600; Lake Tahoe Visitors Center, (916) 573–2674.

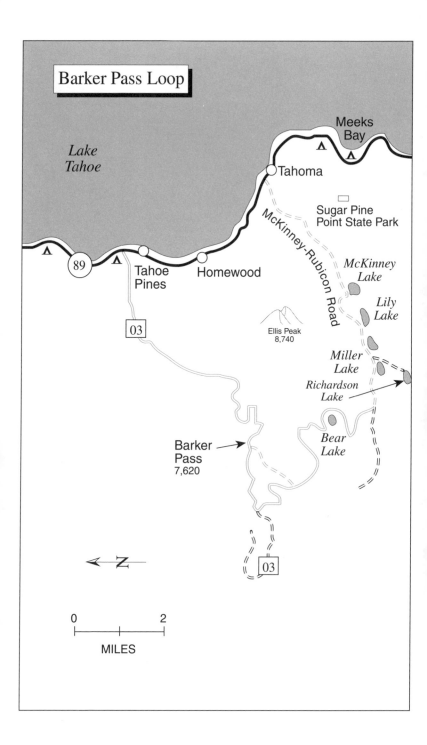

View of Lake Tahoe along the Genoa Peak drive.

The East Fork of the Carson River.

Genoa Peak Vista

LOCATION: Carson Range on the Nevada side of Lake Tahoe, 3.5 miles due east of Cave Rock; north of Nevada 207.

HIGHLIGHTS: Vistas of Tahoe Basin. Genoa Peak, at 9,150 feet, provides a truly stunning top–of–the–world view.

DIFFICULTY: Moderate. The first leg is confusing.

TIME & DISTANCE: 3 hours; about 11 miles.

GETTING THERE: At U.S. 50 and Nevada 207 on the lake's southeastern shore, go east up the Kingsbury Grade on Highway 207 for 2.8 miles, toward Daggett Pass. Turn left, north, onto North Benjamin Drive. The street becomes Andria Drive as it climbs through a residential area. After about 1.7 miles you'll come to a parking area. Set your odometer to 0 here. The drive as I describe it begins on Forest Road 14N32, straight ahead. You can take the drive in the opposite direction.

THE DRIVE: You'll get off to a rough start immediately as the road climbs toward a rock mound. You might use low range for this, but it's not as hard as it looks. At 0.2 mile you'll come to a fork; go left, the easy way. The two routes will reconnect. At 0.7 mile you'll pass a track going left. By 1.3 miles you'll descend into a small basin; go straight, over a hump. At 2.1 miles you'll come to a 3–way fork. To the left is an overlook and great photo opportunity. You want the middle route, marked by one of the orange arrows stuck on pines along the way to denote the route for snowmobilers. At 3.8 miles you'll reach a fork to the right. Genoa Peak rises to the northeast. This 0.7–mile route to the peak is very rough and steep. I recommend an easier route about 0.8 mile farther down the main road. But before going farther you can at this point take the Logan House Loop to the west. Its aspen groves make it a nice autumn alternative. It reconnects to the main road after about 6.5 miles. You'll eventually come out at U.S. 50.

REST STOPS: Genoa Peak. When you're done, visit Sugar Pine Point State Park on the lake's west side.

GETTING HOME: U.S. 50.

MAP: Toiyabe National Forest, Carson Ranger District.

INFORMATION: Tahoe Basin Management Unit, (916) 573–2600; Lake Tahoe Visitors Center, (916) 573–2674.

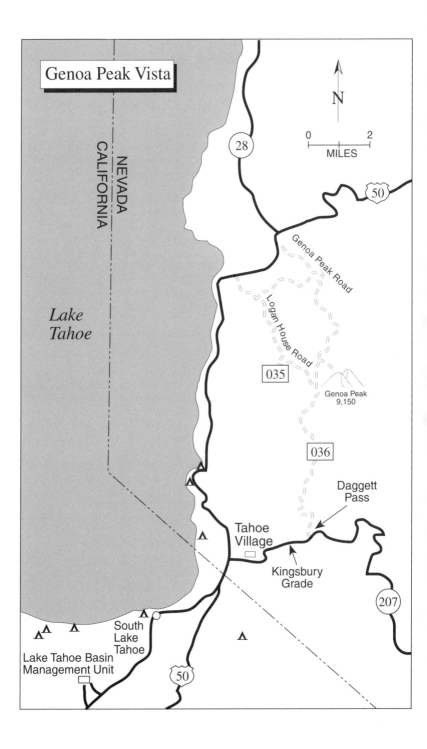

Genoa Peak Vista

NEVADA
CALIFORNIA

Lake
Tahoe

28

50

N

0   2
MILES

Genoa Peak Road

Logan House Road

035

Genoa Peak
9,150

036

Daggett
Pass

Tahoe
Village

Kingsbury
Grade

207

South
Lake
Tahoe

Lake Tahoe Basin
Management Unit

50

Carson River Loop

LOCATION: Along the East Fork of the Carson River in Nevada, between U.S. 395 and the California/Nevada line; 10 miles south of Gardnerville, Nev.

HIGHLIGHTS: A fascinating canyon carved by the river, which is being considered for federal protection as wild and scenic.

DIFFICULTY: Mostly easy to moderate, with a difficult stretch as you climb out of the canyon.

TIME & DISTANCE: About 2.5 hours; almost 12 miles.

GETTING THERE: You can take this drive in either direction. I describe it beginning on Leviathan Mine Road, a west turn off U.S. 395 almost 10 miles south of Pinenut Road, at Gardnerville's south end. If you want to go in the other direction, turn west off U.S. 395 onto Forest Road 189 about 4.7 miles south of Pinenut Road, just past the sign on the right that says "China Springs Facility." Set your odometer to 0.

THE DRIVE: Leviathan Mine Road, FR 052, is a good unpaved road going west from U.S. 395 across Double Spring Flat. Much of this drive will take you past large areas of brush and trees that burned in 1985. At 1.9 miles from the highway, turn right onto two–track FR 189. It's quite rocky as you descend into a canyon. You'll pass through a small pasture and go by a spring. Watch for cattle. At 4 miles you'll come to a fork. Go right. At 5 miles there's a narrow bridge across an irrigation ditch. Cross it, and soon you'll be driving along the side of a canyon. You'll see the river; head toward it. Follow the river downstream. After turning away from the river, you'll need to use low range as you climb almost 700 feet out of the canyon. There are some rocky stretches, and one stretch that will make your vehicle lean. Take it slow. Once out of the canyon, you'll get a nice view of the Sierras. Drive north across the flats. Eventually you'll come out on a graded dirt road. Go left, and you'll soon end up at U.S. 395.

REST STOPS: Some primitive campsites on a nice beach in the canyon among some trees. You can't miss it. A good place to turn the kids loose for a while, have lunch, relax, etc.

GETTING HOME: U.S. 395 north or south.

MAP: Toiyabe National Forest, Carson Ranger District.

INFORMATION: Carson District, (702) 882–2766.

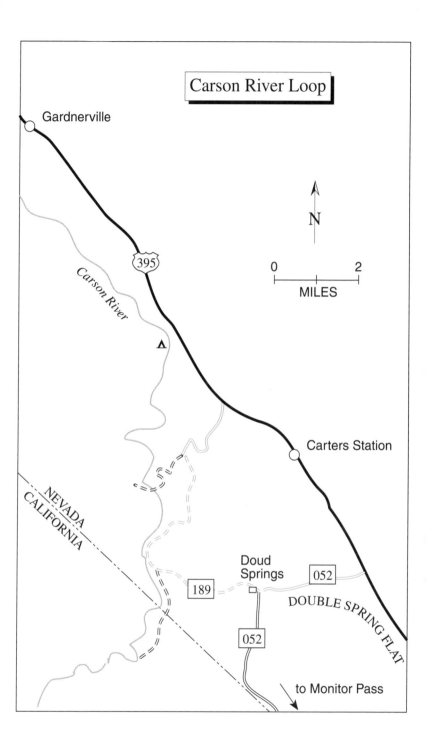

Carson River Loop

Gardnerville

N

0   2
MILES

395

Carson River

Carters Station

NEVADA
CALIFORNIA

Doud
Springs

052

189

DOUBLE SPRING FLAT

052

to Monitor Pass

The summit along the Blue Lakes Loop.

Caples Lake, on the way to the overlook.

Blue Lakes Loop

LOCATION: Alpine County south of Carson Pass and state Highway 88.

HIGHLIGHTS: Vistas of the high peaks in the Mokelumne Wilderness, high meadows, hiking, lakes.

DIFFICULTY: Easy to moderate. The single–lane road along a ledge leading to the 8,800–foot summit might raise some eyebrows.

TIME & DISTANCE: 3 hours and about 20 miles, depending on whether you hike down to the basin at the summit, take photos, savor the sweet air, etc.

GETTING THERE: This can be taken in either direction, but either way begins at Highway 88. I'll describe it from the eastern tip of Red Lake, just east of Carson Pass. Take the Red Lake turnoff, then the left fork through a large green gate. Set your odometer to 0 there. You'll be on Forest Road 013.

THE DRIVE: At 1.5 miles you'll cross a small bridge over Forestdale Creek. The road is good with glimpses of high peaks. You'll see a sign stating that Lost Lakes is 3 miles, and Upper Blue Lakes 4. A short distance farther you'll come to a fork; go right. The road will climb, becoming a single lane at 1.9 miles. By 3 miles you're at the summit, where you'll follow a segment of the Pacific Crest National Scenic Trail. You can hike down to the pristine glacial bowl below. But be forewarned: I've found a large snowbank blocking the road here in mid–August. (Usually it's clear by mid–July.) You'll descend toward Blue Lakes. The short spur to pretty Lost Lakes is worth taking. There are some fairly steep stretches beyond the Lost Lakes turnoff as you drive through forest to Upper Blue Lake. There are also spurs toward Meadow and Twin lakes. Don't try the extremely rough trail south along Blue Creek. At the southern tip of Lower Blue Lake turn east and then north for the scenic 12–mile drive back to Highway 88.

REST STOPS: Picnicking at Lost Lakes; developed campgrounds with toilets along Upper and Lower Blue Lakes, and in Hope Valley near Highway 88.

GETTING HOME: Highway 88 west toward Stockton, or east and north toward U.S. 395, Carson City and Reno; or Highway 89 north to Lake Tahoe, Truckee and Interstate 80.

MAP: Eldorado National Forest.

INFORMATION: Amador Ranger District, (209) 295–4251. There's an information center at Carson Pass, where you can get maps.

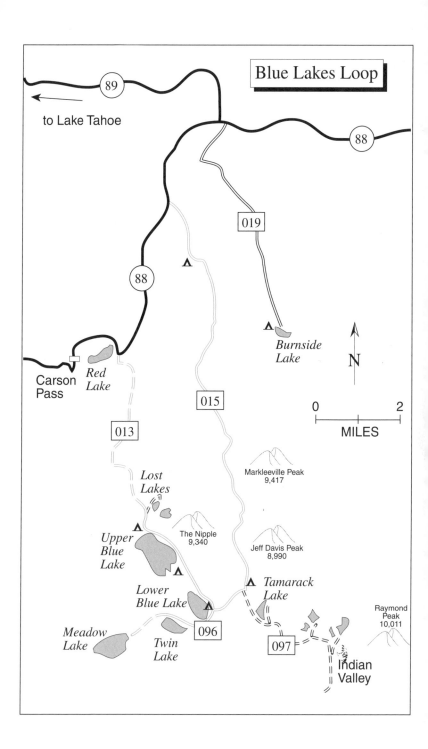

Blue Lakes Loop

89

to Lake Tahoe

88

019

88

Burnside
Lake

N

0   2
MILES

Carson
Pass

Red
Lake

013

015

Markleeville Peak
9,417

Lost
Lakes

The Nipple
9,340

Jeff Davis Peak
8,990

Upper
Blue
Lake

Tamarack
Lake

Raymond
Peak
10,011

Lower
Blue Lake

Meadow
Lake

Twin
Lake

096

097

Indian
Valley

Indian Valley

LOCATION: Alpine County, south of state Highway 88 and about 10 miles straight southeast of Carson Pass.

HIGHLIGHTS: Pretty lakes and meadows, high craggy peaks, stream crossings.

DIFFICULTY: Easy, with a moderate spot or two.

TIME & DISTANCE: About 3 hours and 38 miles round–trip from Highway 88. Not a loop.

GETTING THERE: 4 miles east of Red Lake on Highway 88, turn south on the paved road to Blue Lakes. About 7 miles later the road will become fairly rough but easy gravel and rock. At about 9.4 miles from the highway turn left at the sign to Tamarack Lake and Wet Meadow on Forest Road 097.

THE DRIVE: In less than a mile you'll get a great view of high peaks. The road is washboarded dirt. Soon you'll come to a T intersection. Set your odometer to 0 here. Lower Sunset Lake, about 1.5 miles to the left, is a pretty little lake. But the real beauty lies to the right. Go up a short four–wheel drive stretch, and you'll soon be in magnificent, lush Indian Valley. After 0.4 mile a left fork will take you a half mile to Wet Meadows Reservoir, which has some beautiful mountain scenery around it. It's worth the jaunt. Go right, and you'll enter the gorgeous valley. The highest peak to the east, Raymond Peak, rises to 10,011 feet. (You're at about 8,000 feet.) Soon you'll cross an easy little stream, but a short distance later there's a bit more challenging crossing. Scout out the alternatives; stay out of anything that might be too muddy. This is sensitive ground; don't make a new trail. Cross another little stream after that and go up some rocks, a good spot for photos. The road ends about 0.7 miles farther at the Mokelumne Wilderness boundary, a fine place for primitive camping.

REST STOPS: Nice lakes for picnicking. Lots of campsites, but no facilities. Developed campgrounds at Upper and Lower Blue Lakes, farther down the Blue Lakes Road.

GETTING HOME: Return the way you came. Or if you have about two more hours to spare, do the Blue Lakes Loop.

MAP: Toiyabe National Forest, Carson Ranger District. You can buy maps at an information center on Carson Pass.

INFORMATION: Carson District, (702) 882–2766.

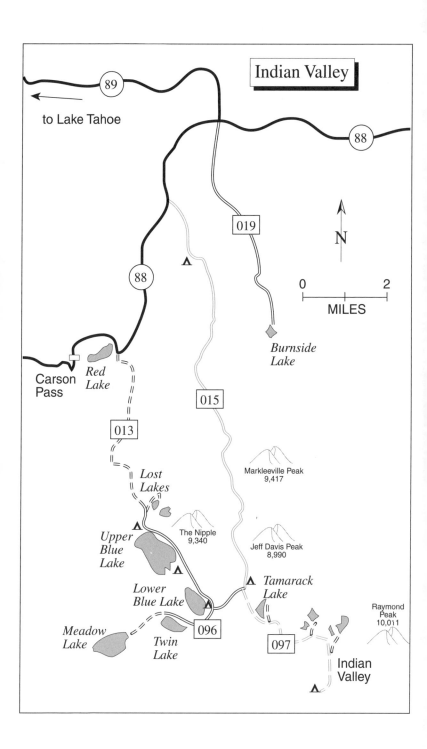

Indian Valley

89

to Lake Tahoe

88

019

N

0   2
MILES

88

Carson
Pass

Red
Lake

Burnside
Lake

013

015

Lost
Lakes

Markleeville Peak
9,417

Upper
Blue
Lake

The Nipple
9,340

Jeff Davis Peak
8,990

Tamarack
Lake

Raymond
Peak
10,011

Lower
Blue Lake

Meadow
Lake

Twin
Lake

096

097

Indian
Valley

Burnside Lake

LOCATION: Alpine County south of state Highway 88 at the Highway 89 turnoff to Lake Tahoe.

HIGHLIGHTS: A pretty, quiet lake that makes a nice side trip. A spur towards Pickett Peak (9,118 ft.) provides great views.

DIFFICULTY: Easy.

TIME & DISTANCE: 1.5 hours and almost 15 miles round–trip. This is not a loop.

GETTING THERE: At the Highway 89 turnoff north to Lake Tahoe, turn south off Highway 88 onto dirt Burnside Lake Road, Forest Road 019. Set your odometer to 0.

THE DRIVE: You'll climb through aspens and pines, getting glimpses of mountains that may still have snow. At 2.7 miles you'll pass FR 053 to the left. Take it, and after about 1.2 miles you'll see a little fork to the left. It'll take you to a turnaround that forms a very good overlook with views from about 8,200 feet. Back on FR 019, go left and you'll be at the lake in less than 3 miles.

REST STOPS: The lake has primitive camping, and is a nice place for lunch.

GETTING HOME: Highway 88 west toward Stockton, or east and north toward U.S. 395, Carson City and Reno; or Highway 89 north to Lake Tahoe, Truckee and Interstate 80.

MAP: Toiyabe National Forest, Carson Ranger District.

INFORMATION: Carson District, (702) 882–2766.

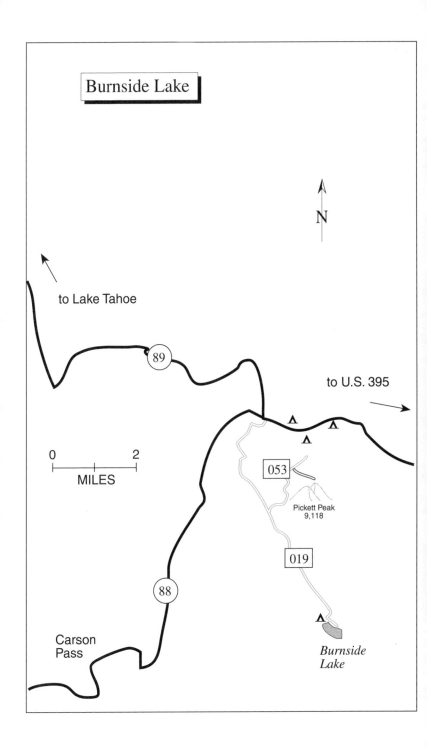

Burnside Lake

N

to Lake Tahoe

89

to U.S. 395

0   2
MILES

053

Pickett Peak
9,118

019

Carson
Pass

88

Burnside
Lake

Caples Lake Overlook

LOCATION: El Dorado & Alpine counties; north of Caples Lake and Highway 88, and about 16 miles due south of Lake Tahoe.

HIGHLIGHTS: A mix of pastoral and high Sierra scenes.

DIFFICULTY: Easy to moderate, with a stream crossing I'll rate moderate.

TIME & DISTANCE: 4 hours and 7.5 miles round–trip. This is not a loop.

GETTING THERE: About 0.7 mile east of the Caples Lake dam, turn north from Highway 88 onto paved Schneider Cow Camp Road and set your odometer to 0.

THE DRIVE: Drive into the Caltrans maintenance station, then turn left among some buildings. The dirt road begins immediately past the maintenance station. Go right. You're at about 8,100 feet now. You'll pass some cliffs on the right as you drive on a road salted with bits of granite. By 1.5 miles you'll pass a pretty meadow and a barn to the left. Then you'll see a sign saying four–wheel drive only. After going through the fence the road becomes quite rough, but still easy. At about 2.3 miles you'll come to a brook with a steep bank on the other side. You might have to take the time to toss some rocks in the holes on the other side dug by the spinning tires of people who went before you. That'll give you better traction. The road then climbs through meadows with flowers and great views of the basin of Caples Lake and Kirkwood ski area. At about 3.1 miles you'll come to a summit, more than 8,500 feet high, and a granite outcrop on the left that'll give you a sweeping view. Beyond that is a slow, rough trail to Highway 50 that I don't recommend.

REST STOPS: Refresh at historic Kirkwood Inn before or after the drive. Campgrounds around Caples Lake, and primitive campsites in the meadow with the old barn you'll pass, as well as on the approach to the overlook and at the overlook. Caples Lake Resort (209–258–8888) has rooms, cabins, restaurant, etc.

GETTING HOME: Go back to Highway 88.

MAP: Eldorado National Forest.

INFORMATION: Amador District, (209) 295–4251.

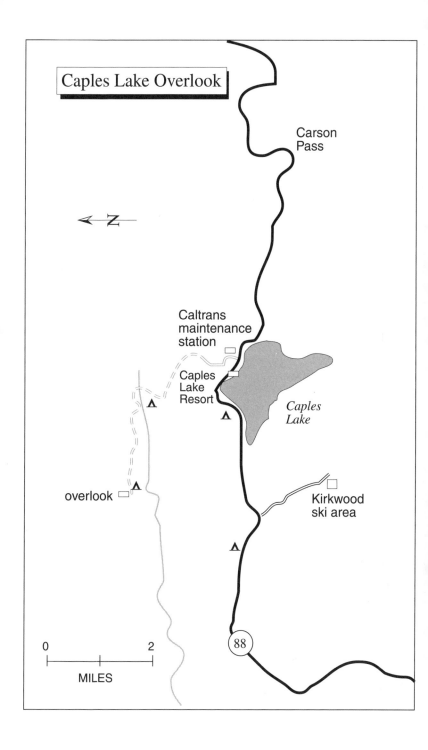

Caples Lake Overlook

Carson Pass

Caltrans maintenance station

Caples Lake Resort

Caples Lake

overlook

Kirkwood ski area

0 — 2

MILES

88

Photo by Peter Huegel

Viewing the Mokelumne Wilderness from Pardoes Road.

Antelope Valley, Nev., from the Virgil Connell Spring Loop.

Pardoes Road

LOCATION: Amador County; southeast of scenic state Highway 88, and south of Lower Bear River Reservoir.

HIGHLIGHTS: The lake; views of the Mokelumne Wilderness.

DIFFICULTY: Mostly moderate, but if you go far enough there will be some difficult to very difficult moments; many narrow spots among the trees and rocks. Eventually it becomes a serious trail that's not for us. This is not a loop.

TIME & DISTANCE: About 6 to 8 hours and 25 miles round–trip.

GETTING THERE: About 37 miles east of Jackson turn south from Highway 88; it's three miles to Bear River Lake Resort and the lake. A half–mile before the resort, you'll reach a fork. The resort is to the left. After setting your odometer to 0, go straight to begin the drive.

THE DRIVE: It'll take you from 5,800 feet to 8,200 feet in elevation as you drive through pine forest, meadows and past granite outcrops at the edge of the wilderness. Go toward South Shore Campground, on the paved road. Drive along the lake. At about 4.8 miles turn left onto dirt road 8N03F, toward Pardoes Road. At 5.1 the road forks again. Go right, following the orange arrows on the trees (trail markers for snowmobilers). You're on Pardoes Road, and it gets rough soon. At about 7 miles you'll reach a rocky stretch. At about 8.4 miles you can take a track through a meadow on the right, and after a short distance veer left up a short steep pitch to a great picnic spot. About 2 miles farther down the main road you'll come to a fork. Go straight a short distance to a nice vista point. You're over 8,000 feet here. It might be far enough. If you want more, go back to that last fork, turn right and go another 3.3 scenic miles or so — no more — to a granite area where there's primitive camping. But expect some very difficult spots on the way.

REST STOPS: Bear River Lake Resort (209–295–4868) has lodging, camping, boat and canoe rentals, supplies. Swim in the lake. Campground at South Shore. The 30–mile round–trip drive to Salt Springs Reservoir, to the south, is an easy day trip.

GETTING HOME: Highway 88 east or west. Or, from Salt Springs, take Forest Road 9 west for 40 serpentine miles and 2 hours to Highway 88. The latter risks car sickness for the kids.

MAP: Eldorado National Forest.

INFORMATION: Amador District, (209) 295–4251.

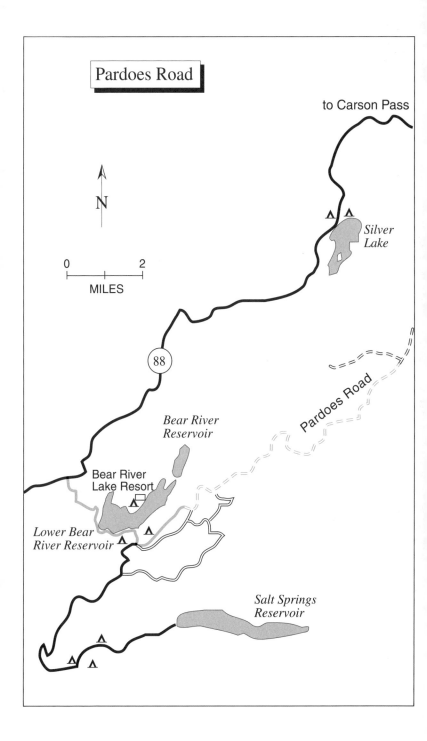

Pardoes Road

to Carson Pass

N

0   2
MILES

88

Silver Lake

Pardoes Road

Bear River Reservoir

Bear River Lake Resort

Lower Bear River Reservoir

Salt Springs Reservoir

Indian Creek Road

LOCATION: Alpine County south of Markleeville, west of state Highway 89/4.

HIGHLIGHTS: Outstanding views of several peaks approaching or exceeding 10,000 feet.

DIFFICULTY: Easy to moderate.

TIME & DISTANCE: 2.5 hours; 16.6 miles round–trip. This is not a loop.

GETTING THERE: Drive south from Markleeville on Highway 89/4 to the Markleeville Campground. Drive another 0.3 mile; turn right (south) on Forest Road 040, and set your odometer to 0.

THE DRIVE: At 0.7 mile from the highway you'll reach a three–way fork; go left. You'll see a sign saying, "Not advised for less than all–wheel drive," which makes it sound harder than it is. The road winds down into a canyon, then climbs to give you views of mountains and canyons. At 3.4 miles you'll reach a spur to the left, which goes 0.4 miles to a primitive campsite and a great overlook to the north and east. Almost 0.6 mile from this spur you'll reach another fork; keep right, as the signpost indicates. In a mile or so you'll be in a logged forested area. In fact, logging here has left some messes. Soon there's another fork; keep left, climbing steeply for a short distance. Eventually you'll emerge from the trees to be greeted by a spectacular view of high Sierra peaks. After 0.7 mile you'll reach another fork; keep left. Follow the two–track down, and the road will end in a logged clearing about 0.4 mile farther. There are more great views and a turnaround here.

REST STOPS: The overlook early in the trip, and a knoll with a great view to the northeast, about 6.6 miles into the drive.

GETTING HOME: Highway 89/4 north to Highway 88, or southwest toward Angels Camp.

MAP: Toiyabe National Forest, Carson Ranger District.

INFORMATION: Carson District, (702) 882–2766.

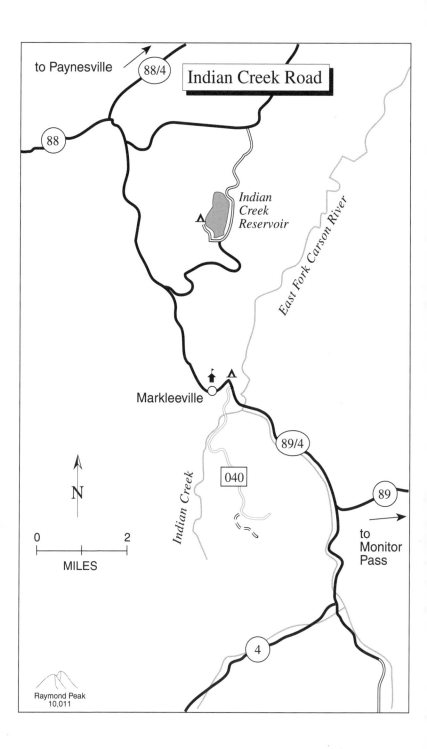

to Paynesville

Indian Creek Road

Indian Creek Reservoir

East Fork Carson River

Markleeville

Indian Creek

040

89/4

88/4

88

89

to Monitor Pass

4

N

0   2
MILES

Raymond Peak
10,011

Highland Lakes

LOCATION: Alpine County, about 3.5 miles due south of Ebbetts Pass and state Highway 4.

HIGHLIGHTS: Pretty lakes, nice developed campground, wilderness access and hiking, swimming, boating, fishing.

DIFFICULTY: Easy.

TIME & DISTANCE: A little more than an hour and 12.2 miles round–trip. But spend time at the lakes.

GETTING THERE: 1.3 miles west of 8,730–foot Ebbetts Pass, take a sharp turn to the south off Highway 4. The sign might be obscured by brush. Set your odometer to 0.

THE DRIVE: This is a pretty side trip if you're on your way somewhere, or if you're looking for nice place to camp that offers a variety of diversions. After turning off Highway 4 you'll descend on a good dirt road with fine views of peaks and valleys. After about 2.1 miles you'll cross a brook, then a bridge at 3.2 miles. Soon you'll get a great view of cliffs off to the left. Then you'll round a turn and be greeted by a view of tremendous granite peaks ahead. (I've seen them with snow in August.) By 4 miles you'll reach Tryon Meadow, with its rustic ranch buildings and, possibly, some friendly horses loitering in the road. The kids will love it. (You're in the Highland Lakes grazing allotment.) Drive past the buildings, keeping left. Cross another brook, go up a hill, and on the other side you'll descend into Gardener Meadow. Go right at the fork. You're at the lakes, and soon you'll see the nice, shady developed camp-ground on the right. The road ends a short distance farther at a trailhead and entry point for the Carson–Iceberg Wilderness.

REST STOPS: Lots of nice creekside places along the drive for picnics or letting the kids romp. Basic camping at Bloomfield Campground along the drive, or developed camp-ground at Highland Lakes.

GETTING HOME: Highway 4.

MAP: Stanislaus National Forest.

INFORMATION: Calaveras District, (209) 795–1381.

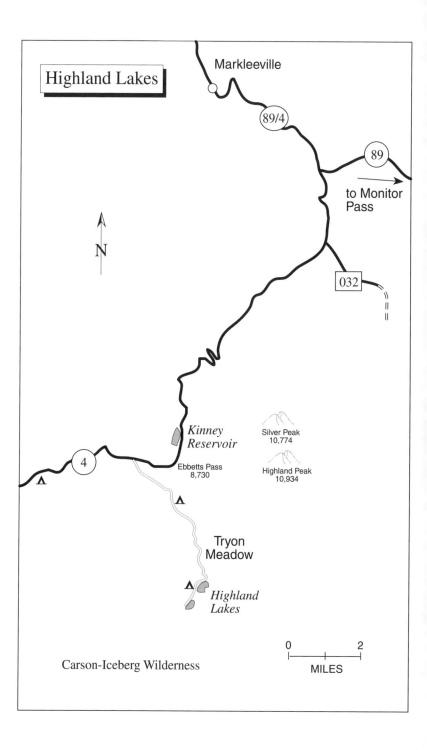

Highland Lakes

Markleeville

89/4

89

to Monitor Pass

N

032

4

Kinney Reservoir

Silver Peak 10,774

Ebbetts Pass 8,730

Highland Peak 10,934

Tryon Meadow

Highland Lakes

Carson-Iceberg Wilderness

0   2
MILES

Leviathan Mine Road

LOCATION: Alpine County about 7 miles due east of Markleeville, north of Highway 89; ends at U.S. 395.

HIGHLIGHTS: The vast open pit sulfur mine's remains and the monumental effort to contain polluted runoff are an amazing and shocking sight in an otherwise beautiful area. The mine is an environmental disaster that continues to pollute nearby streams. The drive will take you through forests, canyons and high–desert mountains.

DIFFICULTY: Easy.

TIME & DISTANCE: About 1.5 hours; 14.5 miles.

GETTING THERE: From Markleeville, drive southeast 5 miles on Highway 89/4. Turn east on Highway 89 at the junction. Drive 4.7 miles, then turn north on Forest Road 052 and set your odometer to 0.

THE DRIVE: FR 052 is a good dirt and gravel road that initially climbs through dry sage and grass hills. (At 1.5 miles from the highway you'll pass, on the left, the turnoff to FR 190 and Haypress Flat, the next trip in this book.) Watch for cattle. The road gets a bit rougher as you descend to the Leviathan Mine gate, at about 7,200 feet elevation. You'll see a sign: "Danger Keep Out; Acid Mine Drainage." Miners began taking copper sulfate from the site in 1863 for processing silver ore at the Comstock Mine at Virginia City, Nev. Off-and-on sulfur mining ceased in 1962, leaving devastation behind. Veer right onto the road that a sign says is not recommended for ordinary cars. It's 12 miles to U.S. 395. Along the way you'll pass a number of spots that give a bird's–eye view of the mine, which is a bizarre sight. Soon you'll pass massive tailing piles. Eventually you'll come to a T intersection; go right. Note the color of the water as you drive along Leviathan Creek on a good road of fine gravel. Soon Leviathan Canyon gives way to a beautiful gorge. You'll pass FR 189, which goes west to the East Fork of the Carson River. Continue north and then east across Double Spring Flat to U.S. 395.

REST STOPS: Visit Markleeville's Alpine County Historical Museum, the 1882 Webster School and the jail cells built in 1865, all on a hill overlooking town. Call (916) 694–2317 for information.

GETTING HOME: U.S. 395 north or south.

MAP: Toiyabe National Forest, Carson Ranger District.

INFORMATION: Carson Ranger District, (702) 882–2766; Markleeville Ranger Station, (916) 694–2911.

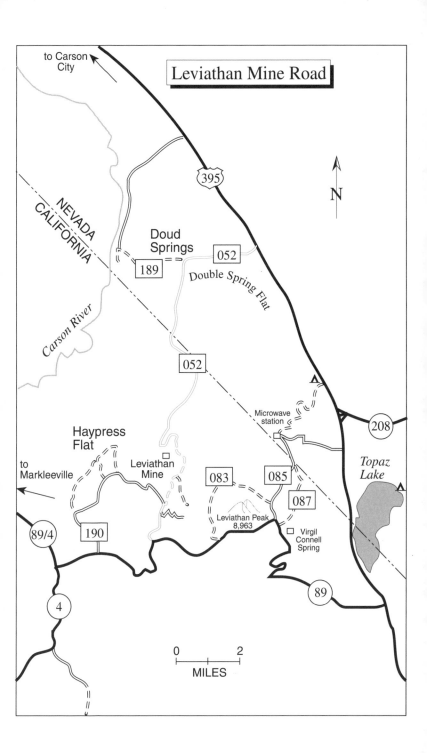

Leviathan Mine Road

to Carson City

NEVADA / CALIFORNIA

Carson River

395

N

Doud Springs

189

052

Double Spring Flat

052

Microwave station

208

Haypress Flat

Leviathan Mine

083

085

087

Topaz Lake

to Markleeville

Leviathan Peak 8,963

Virgil Connell Spring

89/4

190

4

89

0   2
MILES

Haypress Flat Loop

LOCATION: Alpine County north of state Highway 89, east of Markleeville.

HIGHLIGHTS: Varied terrain ranging from craggy canyons to mountain meadows; sweeping vistas; old mines. Many spurs.

DIFFICULTY: Easy; spurs are moderate to difficult.

TIME & DISTANCE: 2.5 hours; about 13 miles, depending on the spurs you take. Go in either direction.

GETTING THERE: About 1.7 miles east of the intersection of state Highways 89 and 4 south of Markleeville, turn north from Highway 89 onto Forest Road 190. Set your odometer to 0.

THE DRIVE: You start out at about 6,300 feet elevation, and climb to over 8,000 feet on old mining roads. You'll climb steeply but easily as you go up Loope Canyon on a good dirt road. FR 326 spurs to the left at the top of the canyon. It's a steep white–knuckle but fun climb up a mountainside. Keep to the left on the way up, and soon you'll come to a dead end with a stupendous view. About a half–mile farther up FR 190, on the left, is a primitive but very nice campsite with a tremendous overlook. But be sure the kids stay away from the fenced open mine shaft nearby. About 0.5 mile farther you'll see the remains of Morningstar Mine on a hillside to the right. Another 1.2 miles farther you'll come to FR 056, heading north. This 4x4 two–track will take you 2.4 miles through sage meadows and aspen groves to Haypress Flat, with more outstanding views of the Sierras. It loops around to bring you back to FR 190. If you take it, veer east after 0.7 miles. Veer south after 0.8 miles. Back on 190, you'll soon descend through conifers. You'll get a peek at the unbelievable site of Leviathan Mine (see drive No. 16). Eventually you'll reach FR 052. Turn right, south, and it's about 1.6 miles to Highway 89.

REST STOPS: No place formal. But that campsite overlook early in the drive is tremendous.

GETTING HOME: Highway 89 east will take you to U.S. 395. Highway 89/4 goes north to Highway 88, and southwest to Angels Camp.

MAP: Toiyabe National Forest, Carson Ranger District.

INFORMATION: Carson District, (702) 882–2766.

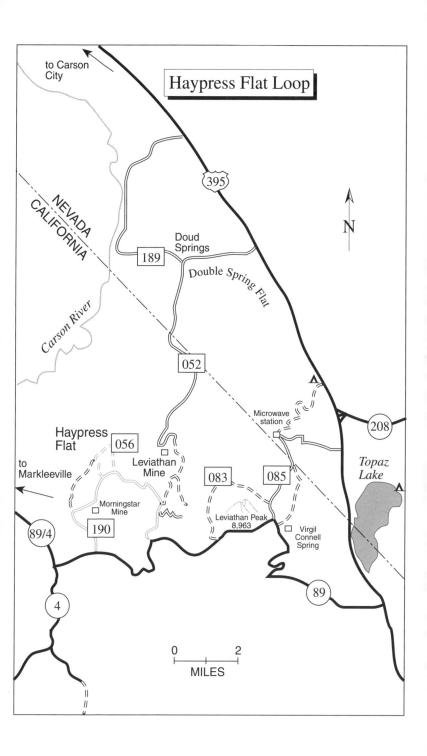

Haypress Flat Loop

to Carson City

NEVADA
CALIFORNIA

Carson River

395

189 Doud Springs

Double Spring Flat

052

N

Microwave station

208

Topaz Lake

Haypress Flat

056

Leviathan Mine

to Markleeville

083

085

190

Morningstar Mine

Leviathan Peak 8,963

Virgil Connell Spring

89/4

4

89

0   2
MILES

TRIP

18

Monitor Pass to U.S. 395

LOCATION: Descends from Monitor Pass on California Highway 89 in Alpine County northeast to U.S. 395 in Nevada.

HIGHLIGHTS: Truly breathtaking 2,600–foot descent from Monitor Pass to Double Spring Flat and U.S. 395.

DIFFICULTY: Easy. Just be careful. Driver must keep his or her eyes on the road while in motion.

TIME & DISTANCE: An hour; 7 miles.

GETTING THERE: From the junction of Highway 89/4, drive east almost 10 miles, crossing Monitor Pass. From U.S. 395, drive west on Highway 89 a little more than 7 miles toward Monitor Pass.

THE DRIVE: If you're looking for an alternate way to get from Highway 89 at Monitor Pass to U.S. 395, this is it. From Highway 89 turn north onto Forest Road 085, a good dirt and gravel road. Set your odometer to 0. You'll pass 8,963–foot Leviathan Peak, to your left. At 2.7 miles, as you pass through sagebrush and grass, you'll cross the Nevada line. You'll see a microwave station up ahead; drive toward it, then turn right when you get there. You'll get a wonderful view of the Carson Valley and U.S. 395 far below. At 3.45 miles you'll pass a fork to the left; go straight, staying on the gravel road. The view is absolutely magnificent as you wind down the mountainside on what becomes a good but single–lane gravel road. You can see Topaz Lake, Antelope Valley, the Pine Nut Mountains and far into Nevada. As with many drives on the abrupt eastern side of the Sierras, this one is not for people who fear heights. Eventually you'll level out and come out at U.S. 395 north of Topaz Lake.

REST STOPS: None, but it's a short and easy drive.

GETTING HOME: U.S. 395 north or south.

MAP: Toiyabe National Forest, Carson Ranger District.

INFORMATION: Carson Ranger District, (702) 882–2766.

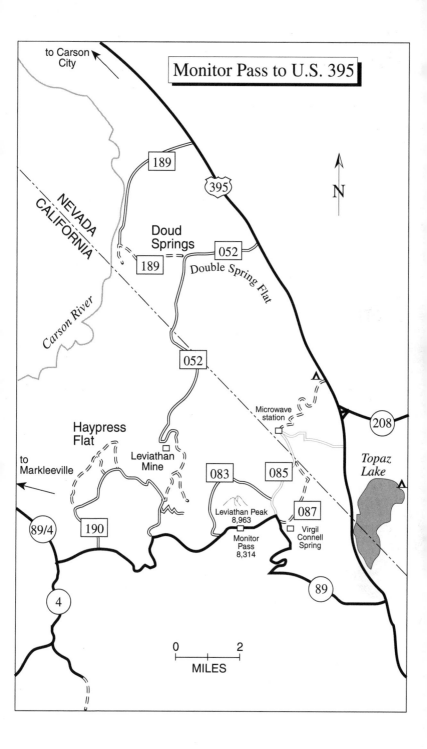

Monitor Pass to U.S. 395

to Carson City

NEVADA / CALIFORNIA

Carson River

189

395

N

Doud Springs

189

052

Double Spring Flat

052

Haypress Flat

Microwave station

208

Topaz Lake

to Markleeville

Leviathan Mine

083

085

089/4

190

Leviathan Peak 8,963

087

Monitor Pass 8,314

Virgil Connell Spring

4

89

0   2
MILES

Virgil Connell Spring Loop

LOCATION: Alpine and Mono counties east of Monitor Pass; north of Highway 89 near the California/Nevada line.

HIGHLIGHTS: Excellent high–elevation views of Nevada's valleys and mountains. A beautiful drive that gives a real sense of what it's like being in the bush. A short drive with good photo opportunities. You might also take the Leviathan Peak Loop (No. 20).

DIFFICULTY: Easy and great fun.

TIME & DISTANCE: An hour; 5.3 miles.

GETTING THERE: About 2 miles east of Monitor Pass, turn north from Highway 89 onto Forest Road 085, a.k.a. the Indian Springs Road, a good gravel road. Set your odometer to 0.

THE DRIVE: Go north on FR 085 for 2.1 miles. Just as the microwave station up ahead comes into view, turn right, or southeast, onto two–track FR 087. Soon you'll pass through grass and sage meadows bordered by aspens and pines. The grass on the road can be quite high, adding to the adventure. About 1.5 miles after leaving FR 085 you'll come to an unmarked fork. The spur to the left goes a short distance to an overlook with a stunning view of Topaz Lake and Antelope Valley to the east, in Nevada. (Elevation at the overlook is about 7,640 ft.) There's an easy turnaround so you can get back to the main trail. About 0.6 miles from the spur is a rocky pitch requiring four–wheel drive. Soon you'll pass Virgil Connell Spring, to the left, and then go over another rocky stretch before coming out on the highway just a few yards from where you went in.

REST STOPS: Anywhere you want, but it's a short drive. The overlook spur is a good one. And take the short drive up FR 057, right off the highway, to within about a quarter mile of the summit of Leviathan Peak. Hike the rest of the way and enjoy the view.

GETTING HOME: Highway 89 east to U.S. 395, or west toward Markleeville and Angels Camp.

MAP: Toiyabe National Forest, Carson Ranger District.

INFORMATION: Carson District, (702) 882–2766.

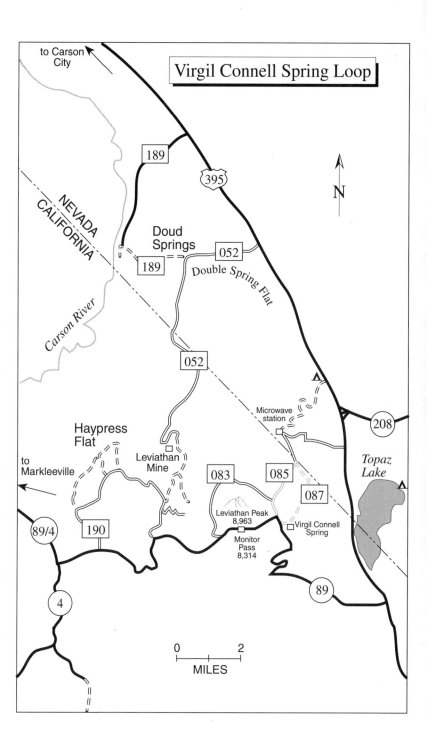

Virgil Connell Spring Loop

to Carson City

189

395

N

NEVADA
CALIFORNIA

Doud Springs

052

189

Double Spring Flat

Carson River

052

Haypress Flat

to Markleeville

Leviathan Mine

Microwave station

083

085

087

208

Topaz Lake

89/4

190

Leviathan Peak 8,963

Virgil Connell Spring

Monitor Pass 8,314

4

89

0   2
MILES

Leviathan Peak Loop

LOCATION: Alpine County at Monitor Pass north of state Highway 89.

HIGHLIGHTS: Outstanding views from the crest of the northern Sierras; a side trip to the summit of Leviathan Peak.

DIFFICULTY: Easy.

TIME & DISTANCE: 1.5 hours; 5.3 miles. Can be taken in either direction.

GETTING THERE: From the junction of Highways 89 and 4, drive east on Highway 89 for 7.6 miles to Monitor Pass. Or if you're driving on U.S. 395, turn west onto Highway 89 just south of Topaz Lake and make the stunning climb about 8 miles to the pass.

THE DRIVE: Turn north off Highway 89 into a sage and grass bowl west of Leviathan Peak (8,963 ft.), where there's a radio relay station. You're going to circle around the base of the peak. The turnoff may not be posted, but you'll be on Forest Road 083. After setting your odometer to 0, follow the two–track to the right of two little ponds toward a saddle between a rocky peak on the left and a rock outcrop on the right. At about 0.6 mile there's a spur to the left, which will go a short distance to a ridge with views of the valley to the west. Soon the main road veers east, at nearly 8,400 feet, giving you fine vistas of Nevada's desert ranges. At 1.8 miles from the highway you'll pass through a large aspen grove. (The aspens here promise a spectacular display of color in early autumn.) At 3.4 miles you'll come to a downhill rock pitch, which may require low–range if you're going in the opposite direction. Take it slow and it's OK. At 3.6 miles you'll come to a fork; go straight. At 3.8 miles you'll pass Big Spring, to your left, as you head south toward the highway. A quarter–mile farther you'll take a track to the left, which will take you a short distance to FR 085. Go right toward the highway, 0.45 mile away.

REST STOPS: Take the short drive up FR 057, off the highway, to within about a quarter mile of the summit of Leviathan Peak. Hike the rest of the way and enjoy the view.

GETTING HOME: Highway 89 east to U.S. 395 or west to Highway 89/4.

MAP: Toiyabe National Forest, Carson Ranger District.

INFORMATION: Carson District, (702) 882–2766.

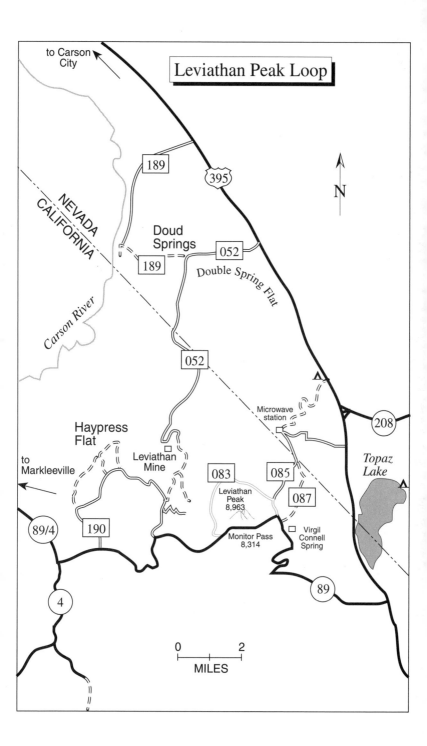

Leviathan Peak Loop

to Carson City

189
395
N

NEVADA
CALIFORNIA

Carson River

Doud Springs
052
189
Double Spring Flat

052

Microwave station

Haypress Flat
Leviathan Mine

083   085
087

Leviathan Peak 8,963

208

Topaz Lake

to Markleeville

89/4   190

Virgil Connell Spring
Monitor Pass 8,314

4

89

0   2
MILES

Risue Road

LOCATION: Northeast of Walker, on U.S. 395; just across the state line in Nevada.

HIGHLIGHTS: Deep, pretty canyons as you climb and then descend through the Sweetwater Mountains east of the Sierras.

DIFFICULTY: Easy. Does not require four–wheel drive.

TIME & DISTANCE: 1 hour; about 16.5 miles.

GETTING THERE: From the east end of Walker, on U.S. 395, drive north on Eastside Road for 8.4 miles. Turn right at the well–marked turnoff for Risue Road, a.k.a. Forest Road 050, and set your odometer to 0.

THE DRIVE: This is a fun, scenic cruise. You'll climb from about 5,460 feet elevation to about 7,300 feet on a good dirt and gravel road. About 1.2 miles after turning off Eastside Road you'll enter Risue Canyon as you follow what likely will be a dry creekbed. By 2.8 miles it becomes a one–lane mountain road. Note the old Arrowhead Mine on the right at 4 miles. You'll do quite a bit of climbing, and at about 6 miles you'll cross a summit of about 7,270 feet. As you descend you'll pass through much heavier vegetation. Soon you'll go along the wall of a deep, rocky and forested canyon. At 7.9 miles you'll come to a turnout. Stop and take in the view. After a short distance you'll reach the northward turnoff for Desert Creek Road, FR 027, and state Highway 338. Stay on Risue Road, and the canyon floor will quickly become something of an oasis with some nice, undeveloped campsites. After you climb out of the canyon, the road will take on the aspect of a roller coaster before you come out on Highway 338.

REST STOPS: Stop along Desert Creek on the canyon floor, after you pass Desert Creek Road. You can camp in an undeveloped site, have lunch, or just let the kids splash in the stream. Bridgeport has a nice little county park, next to the county museum. The beautiful old courthouse, built in 1880, is open to the public.

GETTING HOME: North on Highway 338 to Highway 208, then west to U.S. 395. Or go south on 338 to U.S. 395 and Bridgeport.

MAP: Toiyabe National Forest, Bridgeport Ranger District.

INFORMATION: Bridgeport District, (619) 932–7070.

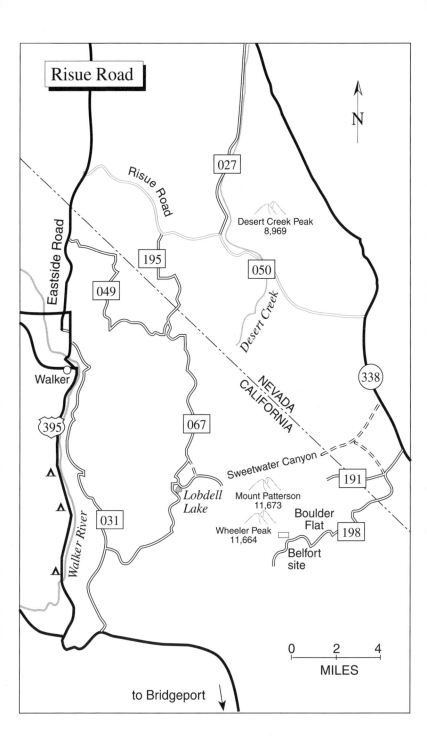

Risue Road

N

027

Risue Road

Desert Creek Peak
8,969

195

050

049

Desert Creek

Eastside Road

NEVADA
CALIFORNIA

338

Walker

067

Sweetwater Canyon

191

395

Lobdell
Lake

Mount Patterson
11,673

Boulder
Flat

198

031

Wheeler Peak
11,664

Belfort
site

Walker River

0   2   4
MILES

to Bridgeport

The Jackass Flat drive.

Southbound on the Fremont-Carson route.

Jackass Flat

LOCATION: Mono County east of Walker, northwest of Bridgeport in the Sweetwater Mountains.

HIGHLIGHTS: Panoramic views of the high Sierras, high–desert meadows, the Three Sisters, exciting driving.

DIFFICULTY: Easy to moderate, with a few difficult spots.

TIME & DISTANCE: 5 hours; about 27 miles. Take in either direction. I describe it going north from U.S. 395.

GETTING THERE: 14.6 miles northwest of Bridgeport, turn north from U.S. 395 onto Forest Road 031. Then turn right, or east, onto FR 067 toward Lobdell Lake. At the southeast corner of the lake, go left, driving 2.5 miles on FR 067 around the west side of the lake and then north of it. Roughly half a mile from where FR 116 branches off to the right, or east, there will be three forks. As the road curves left, or west, away from Desert Creek, a smaller trail continues to the right along the creek. You don't want that, so keep left. Soon you'll see FR 067 branching off up a steep hillside to the right, northward. That's the way. Use low–range gears. You'll climb to the top of a long ridge, driving north.

THE DRIVE: You'll have a sweeping view of the Sierras to the west and the Three Sisters — East Sister (10,402 ft.), Middle Sister (10,859 ft.) and South Sister (11,339 ft.) — to the east. The two–track of loose rock follows a ridge north. After more than 3 miles you'll make a steep descent, using low range, to an intersection visible below. Continue northward through the intersection, following the road around the west side of the hill ahead. Soon you'll cross Jackass Flat. Your road descends from the flats and becomes sandy, soft and nice. You'll come to a corral and water pond at Jackass Spring. Navigate the hole in the road, go through the gate, then when you come to a fork, go left onto FR 195. (There may not be a sign.) As you follow FR 195 you'll cross the Nevada/California line three times. About 8.25 miles from the intersection before Jackass Flat, you'll reach Risue Road. Go left, or west, and follow it 5.1 miles to Eastside Road. Go left to Walker and U.S. 395.

REST STOPS: No place formal. Bridgeport has all services. Visit the old courthouse, county museum and park.

GETTING HOME: U.S. 395 north or south.

MAP: Toiyabe National Forest, Bridgeport Ranger District.

INFORMATION: Bridgeport District, (619) 932–7070.

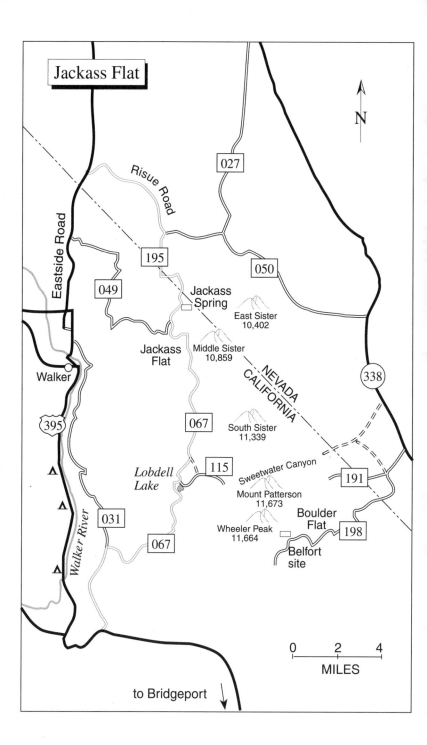

Jackass Flat

N

Risue Road

027

Eastside Road

195

049

050

Jackass Spring

East Sister
10,402

Jackass Flat

Middle Sister
10,859

NEVADA
CALIFORNIA

Walker

395

067

South Sister
11,339

338

Lobdell Lake

115

Sweetwater Canyon

191

Mount Patterson
11,673

031

Boulder Flat

067

Wheeler Peak
11,664

198

Belfort site

Walker River

0   2   4
MILES

to Bridgeport

Fremont-Carson Route

LOCATION: Mono County east of Walker, northwest of Bridgeport; runs parallel to and just east of U.S. 395.

HIGHLIGHTS: Great mountain scenery on this alternative to U.S. 395. You'll climb from below 6,000 feet elevation to over 8,000 feet. I once saw a bear in the road in the middle of the day. In January 1844 explorer Capt. John C. Fremont, guide Kit Carson and a small band of half–starved men passed this way looking for the fabled Ventura River, which they thought would give them easy passage through the high mountains to the west. They ended up forcing their way through in winter instead.

DIFFICULTY: Easy. Does not require four–wheel drive.

TIME & DISTANCE: A leisurely hour or so; 16 miles. Can be taken in either direction.

GETTING THERE: From the east end of Walker, a small town on U.S. 395 south of Topaz Lake, turn north onto paved Eastside Road. Almost 1.2 miles from the highway, turn right, or southeast, onto another paved road. Go 0.2 mile, then veer right again onto dirt Forest Road 031, also called the Burcham Flat Road, and you're on your way. Set your odometer to 0.

THE DRIVE: It starts out as a wide dirt road winding through dry sagebrush canyons. For a while you're in view of U.S. 395, but soon you'll turn into the mountains. The road is loose dirt so you might want to use high–range four–wheel drive for traction. By 6 miles from the highway you're getting outstanding views, especially as you go over a hill and suddenly have the high Sierras appear up ahead. You'll also see several high peaks to the east. Be sure to stop now and then and take in the scenery behind you, too. By 11.6 miles you'll cross a summit at about 8,070 feet. You'll pass the turnoff to Lobdell Lake and other points in the Sweetwater Mountains to the east. Then you'll begin a long, rapid descent on a good dirt road to U.S. 395, at about 7,160 feet elevation. You'll come out 14.6 miles northwest of Bridgeport.

REST STOPS: No place formal. Bridgeport is a neat little town with a small county park. The beautiful old Mono County Courthouse, built in 1880, is still in use and open to the public. There's also the county museum, two blocks from the courthouse and next to the county park.

GETTING HOME: U.S. 395 north or south.

MAP: Toiyabe National Forest, Bridgeport Ranger District.

INFORMATION: Bridgeport District, (619) 932–7070.

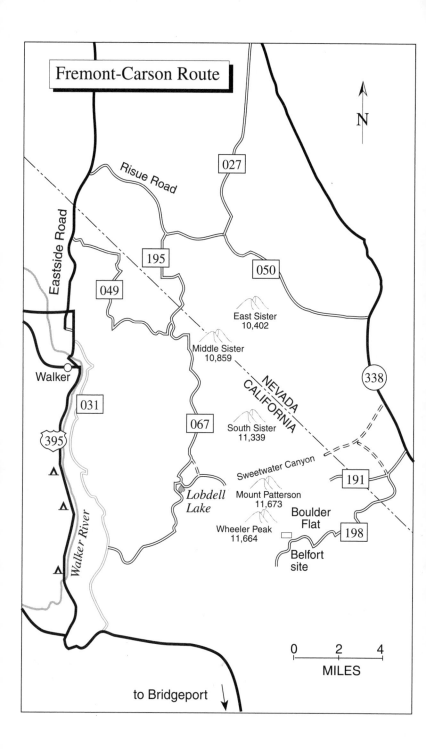

Fremont-Carson Route

Sweetwater Canyon, near Lobdell Lake.

The site of Belfort, at Boulder Flat.

Lobdell Lake

LOCATION: Mono County, in the volcanic Sweetwater Mountains northwest of Bridgeport.

HIGHLIGHTS: High, rolling sage–covered hills. Tremendous views of the Sierras to the southwest. Spur to Sweetwater Canyon.

DIFFICULTY: Easy. Sweetwater Canyon spur is moderate.

TIME & DISTANCE: Round–trip 3 to 3.5 hours; about 21 miles to the lake from U.S. 395, but about 5 miles more round–trip for the dead–end spur up to Sweetwater Canyon to the point where the route is closed.

GETTING THERE: 14.6 miles northwest of Bridgeport on U.S. 395, turn north onto Forest Road 031. Go 4.3 miles; turn east onto FR 067.

THE DRIVE: FR 031 is a very good dirt road that takes you high into the Sweetwaters, a range just east of the Sierras. I like these mountains because they give you views of the Sierras that are harder to get when you're actually in the Sierras. On FR 067 you'll cross some brooks. After passing through a forested stretch you'll suddenly get a great view of Mount Patterson (11,673 ft.) and Wheeler Peak (11,664 ft.). Lobdell Lake, at about 9,140 ft., isn't pretty. The small reservoir is quite sterile looking. To take the spur toward Sweetwater Canyon, veer to the left when you reach the lake. On the northwest corner of the lake turn right onto FR 115. Follow the two–track along a stream, eventually crossing it to the right. Beyond are some deep ruts and rocky stretches to negotiate. I recommend low range. You'll reach a couple of crests; take in the view behind you. Continue on for more spectacular views of Patterson and Wheeler. Eventually you'll see a sign on a tree, at a creek, that says the route is closed beyond this point to motorized travel, although you can hike if you want. Turn around here.

REST STOPS: Nothing formal. I recommend lunch at one of the crests you go over on the Sweetwater Canyon spur. In Bridgeport, visit the old courthouse, built in 1880 and still in use; and the Mono County Museum next to the county park, where you can have lunch and let the kids loose.

GETTING HOME: Backtrack to U.S. 395, or continue on the Jackass Flat drive.

MAP: Toiyabe National Forest, Bridgeport Ranger District.

INFORMATION: Bridgeport District, (619) 932–7070.

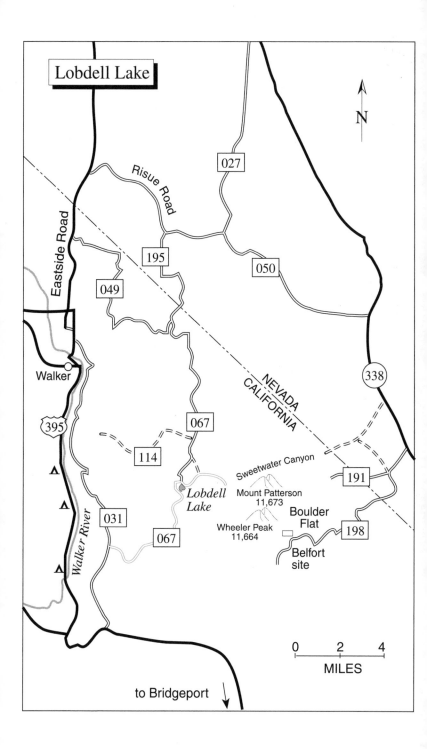

Lobdell Lake

Boulder Flat

LOCATION: Mono County 11 miles due north of Bridgeport, on U.S. 395. In the Sweetwater Mountains west of Nevada Highway 338 and the California/Nevada line.

HIGHLIGHTS: Stunning views as you climb from 6,730 feet to almost 10,800 feet; remains of Belfort, a high–elevation settlement in a once–thriving gold and silver mining district.

DIFFICULTY: Moderate. A climb at the end can seem difficult. The climb to Boulder Flat along the narrow mountainside road is hair–raising but easy. Take it slow.

TIME & DISTANCE: 4 hours, 22 miles round–trip. This is not a loop.

GETTING THERE: From Bridgeport, go north on state Highway 182. About 6 miles after crossing the Nevada line, when the highway becomes Nevada 338, turn southwest at Sweetwater Ranch onto Forest Road 191. Set your odometer at 0 when you pull off the highway. Veer left, and be considerate as you pass through the ranch. At 1.1 miles from the highway go left onto FR 198 to Frying Pan Creek. At 4.9 miles from the highway, FR 198 turns west toward the mountains.

THE DRIVE: Some of the peaks you'll see are well over 11,000 feet high. After you turn right at mile 4.9, you'll begin a slow, rocky climb using low–range gears. At 7.1 miles you'll reach a clearing where Star City used to be, at about 8,740 feet. Get out and look back. Up ahead you'll see the mountainside road you'll take. Soon you'll be creeping along, making a fairly easy but quite exciting climb. At the end is pretty Boulder Flat, a basin at the foot of 11,664–foot Wheeler Peak. You'll find some old log buildings and foundations, all that remain of Belfort. (Don't take anything.) You're at about 10,300 feet. Go through the trees to the left. You'll climb again, and then cross a field of sagebrush and rock. Head directly toward the cirque up ahead. Go down some switchbacks, then enter a beautiful pass where you'll follow a brook to a meadow. At the meadow go left across the brook. The steep route you'll see ahead isn't as hard as it looks. Use low range, go slow, keep the throttle steady and keep moving. At the top, at about 10,780 feet, you'll get a tremendous view of the Sierra Nevada. Turn around here, and use low–range gears going down the hill.

REST STOPS: Belfort. There are primitive campsites in the trees toward the base of the mountain.

GETTING HOME: Retrace your route.

MAP: Toiyabe National Forest, Bridgeport District.

INFORMATION: Bridgeport District, (619) 932–7070.

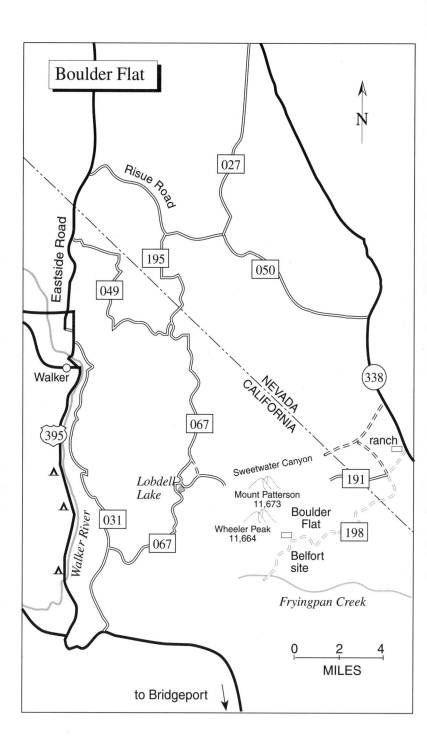

Boulder Flat

Inspecting Chemung Mine, along the Ghost Town Loop.

Relaxing in an aspen grove along the Laurel Lakes drive.

Ghost Town Loop

LOCATION: Mono County, in the Bodie Hills between U.S. 395 and the California/Nevada line, east of Bridgeport.

HIGHLIGHTS: This drive takes you deep into the rolling Bodie Hills, giving views of the Sierras to the west. It takes in the remains of an old mining region, including the ghost towns of Masonic and Bodie. You'll drive the scenic back way into Bodie, avoiding both heavy tourist traffic and the $5 entry fee into the West's best–preserved ghost town, now a state park.

DIFFICULTY: Easy. I describe it from Bridgeport north, east, then south to Bodie. You can go in the opposite direction.

TIME & DISTANCE: 3 leisurely hours or less, 32 miles.

GETTING THERE: From the U.S. 395/California Highway 182 intersection at Bridgeport, go north on Highway 182 about 3.8 miles. Turn east onto Forest Road 046, a.k.a. Masonic Road, and set your odometer to 0.

THE DRIVE: After 5 miles you'll pass the ruins of Chemung Mine on the right as you circle around 9,217–foot Masonic Mountain. This scenic stretch provides views of a wide range of geologic features as it climbs to a saddle at 8,760 feet. At 7.7 miles from the highway you'll reach a 1.2–mile spur to the right that will take you up to a radio relay tower atop Masonic Mountain, where there's an outstanding 360–degree vista. Soon you'll reach FR 169 at the site of old Upper Town. Go left, north, through a canyon. In about a mile you'll see what's left of Masonic alongside the road, and of mines on the hillsides. The town, founded at the turn of the century, stemmed from an 1860 gold find. It grew into three sections: Upper, Middle (Masonic) and Lower Town. But the gold didn't follow any pattern, and ran out. Scavengers have hauled off most of the towns' remains over the years. From Masonic, return to the intersection at Upper Town. Continue south on FR 169, the Bodie–Masonic Road. Go almost 14 miles. You'll round a turn and look down on Bodie, which once had 10,000 residents.

REST STOPS: 1.6 miles south of the intersection of roads 169 and 168 is a spur to the east. It goes down to another old mine, but shortly after turning onto the spur there's a nice aspen grove on the right. Tour Bodie.

GETTING HOME: Go west from Bodie 13 miles on state Highway 270 to U.S. 395. Avoid the Cottonwood Canyon road.

MAP: Toiyabe National Forest, Bridgeport Ranger District.

INFORMATION: Bridgeport District, (619) 932–7070; Bodie State Historic Park, (619) 647–6445.

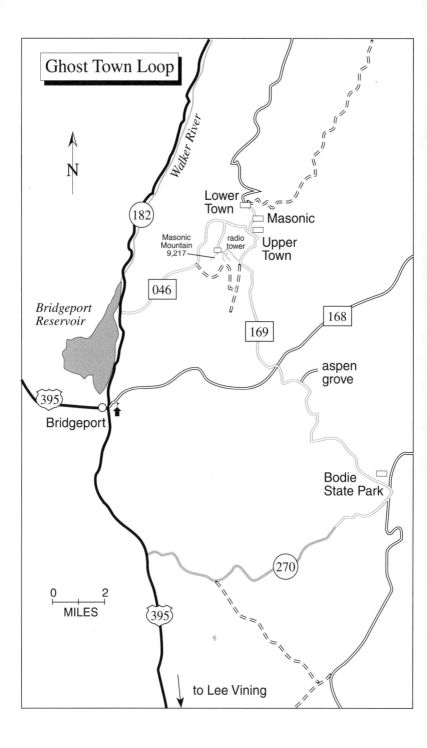

Ghost Town Loop

N

Walker River

182

Masonic Mountain 9,217

radio tower

Lower Town

Masonic

Upper Town

046

169

168

Bridgeport Reservoir

aspen grove

395

Bridgeport

Bodie State Park

0   2
MILES

270

395

to Lee Vining

Summers Meadows

LOCATION: Mono County south of Bridgeport, west of U.S. 395.

HIGHLIGHTS: Lots of aspens, making it a fine early autumn drive; lovely meadows; excellent views of the high Sierra.

DIFFICULTY: Easy. There's only one minor spot where four–wheel drive will be useful. It's a real nice side trip if you're on your way somewhere on U.S. 395.

TIME & DISTANCE: An hour and 15 miles. Can easily be combined with the Dunderberg Meadow Road (No. 28) and the Copper Mountain Loop (No. 29).

GETTING THERE: About 4.5 miles south of Bridgeport, turn east from U.S. 395 onto Forest Road 142. You'll see a small white bridge and a historical marker, which tells of a "poor farm," a refuge for the aged, ill and penniless, that stood in a nearby meadow in the late 1880s. Set your odometer to 0 here.

THE DRIVE: You'll wind south and west through sagebrush on a good dirt road toward the mountains. At 0.9 miles from the highway, turn west onto FR 144, the Summers Meadows Road. At almost 3 miles you'll pass a lush meadow on the right. You'll weave in and out of federal Bureau of Land Management, U.S. Forest Service and private land. At about 4.2 miles you'll get some fabulous views as you enter a canyon. At 7.4 miles it starts getting rougher, and you'll climb more steeply using four–wheel drive. Soon you'll reach an open area with an old shack on the right. Turn around here. The brush on the road up ahead will do dreadful things to your SUV's paint.

REST STOPS: About 2.3 miles from the highway, at a bridge, there's a pretty camping and picnicking area in an aspen grove beside Green Creek. The kids will love it.

GETTING HOME: Return to U.S. 395.

MAP: Toiyabe National Forest, Bridgeport Ranger District.

INFORMATION: Bridgeport District, (619) 932–7070.

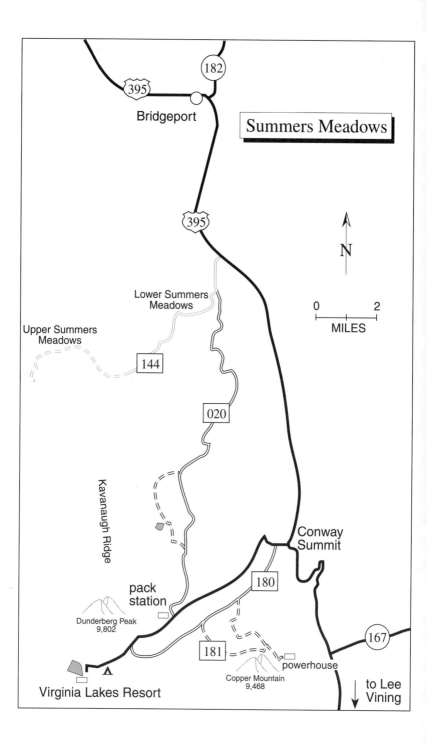

Summers Meadows

Dunderberg Meadow Road

LOCATION: Mono County northwest of Mono Lake, near the Hoover Wilderness.

HIGHLIGHTS: Very scenic, with many aspen groves and high peaks that make it a great early autumn drive. There's a gorgeous unnamed lake at about 10,250 feet on a spur toward Kavanaugh Ridge. This is a great alternate if you're heading somewhere on U.S. 395 and have some extra time. It can be combined with the Copper Mountain Loop (No. 29) and Summers Meadows (No. 27).

DIFFICULTY: An easy, very pleasant drive. The spur to the lake is moderate. The entire drive can be taken in either direction, but I think going north, the direction in which I describe it, is the most scenic.

TIME & DISTANCE: 2 hours, 15 miles.

GETTING THERE: From 8,138–foot Conway Summit, the highest point on U.S. 395 about 12 miles north of Lee Vining, turn west on the Virginia Lakes Road. After about 4.5 miles turn right, north, on Forest Road 020 toward Green Creek. Set your odometer to 0.

THE DRIVE: FR 020, the Dunderberg Meadow Road, begins as a good gravel, two–lane road. In less than a mile it narrows to a single lane, then winds through pines and across sage and grass foothills. You'll come to a fork at FR 178, 1.6 miles from where you left the Virginia Lakes Road. Stay on the main road, and 0.3 mile farther turn left. The two turnoffs end up at a pretty lake at the base of Kavanaugh Ridge, but this second turnoff is easier. From the lake backtrack to the main road, and continue north. You'll begin descending rapidly, passing a large grassy meadow on the right with rock outcrops. On your left will be aspen groves and high peaks. Eventually you'll come to the other end of FR 178, up a beautiful valley. But it's too rough. Soon FR 020 joins FR 142 and, in 3.4 miles, ends at U.S. 395.

REST STOPS: The unnamed lake is an outstanding place for a break. Lee Vining has all services. (I liked the Yosemite Trails Inn restaurant.) You can also take in the ghost town of Bodie. There's a nice park north of Lee Vining, just off U.S. 395 on the northwest shore of Mono Lake. But watch out for yellow jackets.

GETTING HOME: U.S. 395 north or south.

MAP: Toiyabe National Forest, Bridgeport District.

INFORMATION: Bridgeport District, (619) 932–7070.

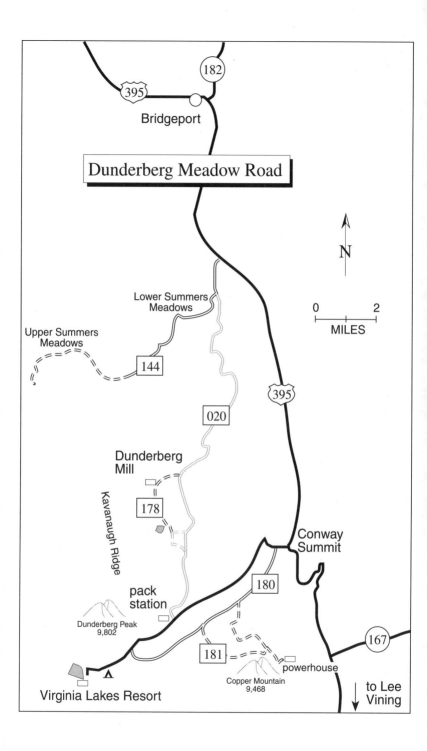

182

395

Bridgeport

Dunderberg Meadow Road

N

0   2
MILES

395

Lower Summers
Meadows

Upper Summers
Meadows

144

020

Dunderberg
Mill

Kavanaugh Ridge

178

Conway
Summit

pack
station

180

Dunderberg Peak
9,802

167

181

powerhouse

Copper Mountain
9,468

Virginia Lakes Resort

to Lee
Vining

Copper Mountain Loop

LOCATION: Mono County, west of U.S. 395 at Conway Summit.

HIGHLIGHTS: Contrast of Mono Basin and Sierra peaks.

DIFFICULTY: Easy.

TIME & DISTANCE: 2 hours, 10 miles. Can be combined with the Dunderberg Meadow Road (No. 28) and Summers Meadows (No. 27).

GETTING THERE: At 8,138–foot Conway Summit, the highest point on U.S. 395, 12 miles north of Lee Vining, turn west on Virginia Lakes Road. At 0.45 mile from the highway, turn south onto Forest Road 180. A sign says "Jordan Basin." Set your odometer to 0.

THE DRIVE: The road quickly becomes rocky as you drive along a steep mountain slope. But you won't need four–wheel drive. In no time you'll get panoramic views of Mono Lake (one of the oldest bodies of water in North America), Mono Craters and other features formed over millions of years by glaciation, volcanic eruptions and faulting. You'll also have great views of high Sierra peaks. About 1.5 miles from where you turned onto FR 180, you'll come to a left fork onto FR 181. Take it. Soon you'll cross a wide grass and sage meadow. At just over 4 miles you'll take a hard right up a short rise. As you go over the top you'll have a heart–stopping view of massive Tioga Crest and glacial Lundy Canyon. You'll cross a clearing, wind through trees, crawl over rocks, and be rewarded with more sweeping views of those incredible peaks. Once out of the trees you'll cross an open area strewn with rocks. You can see the trail up ahead. Eventually you'll make a hard right again, then descend rapidly (you're at about 9,600 feet) across the top of that same broad meadow you crossed earlier, ending up back in the trees. Soon you'll reach FR 180 again. You'll enter private property if you go left, so go right and return to the Virginia Lakes Road.

REST STOPS: Lee Vining; the visitors center at Mono Lake, north of town on the highway; picnicking, bird watching, a playground and restrooms at a county park off U.S. 395 on Mono Lake's northwestern tip. In town, try Yosemite Trails Inn restaurant.

GETTING HOME: U.S. 395 north or south, or Tioga Road into Yosemite National Park.

MAP: Toiyabe National Forest, Bridgeport Ranger District.

INFORMATION: Bridgeport District, (619) 932–7070.

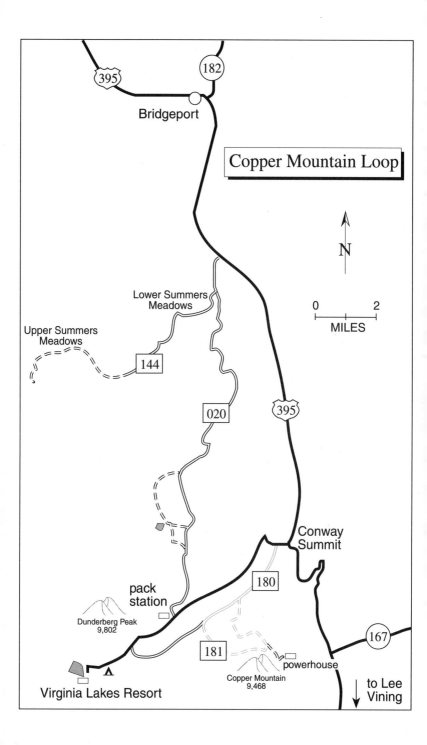

Taking in the view along the Laurel Lakes drive.

Photo by Peter Huegel

Camping at Laurel Lakes.

Laurel Lakes

LOCATION: Mono County south of the Mammoth Lakes turnoff from U.S. 395; about 6 miles southeast of Mammoth Lakes.

HIGHLIGHTS: An outstanding autumn drive if you're visiting the Mammoth Lakes/Mono Lake area. It features a beautiful climb up a glacial moraine into a valley. There are many aspens, making it a gorgeous drive in early October. The road ends at a pair of pretty lakes near the John Muir Wilderness. Varied road conditions add to the interest.

DIFFICULTY: Easy. A tricky turnaround at the end.

TIME & DISTANCE: 3 hours and less than 12 miles round–trip from U.S. 395. This is not a loop.

GETTING THERE: About a mile southeast of the Mammoth Lakes turnoff on U.S. 395, turn south onto the Sherwin Creek Road. Drive southwest for 1.3 miles to Laurel Canyon Road. (The sign may be fallen down or turned around.) Set your odometer at 0, and take that road south. You're at about 7,400 feet elevation here, and you'll climb as high as 9,800 feet, ultimately ending at about 9,700 feet at the lakes.

THE DRIVE: About a half–mile after going up a switchback you'll pass through an aspen grove. About 3 miles from the Laurel Canyon Road turnoff you'll climb more switchbacks. From there you'll get a view of Laurel Creek cascading through aspen groves. Soon you'll get a great view of peaks of the John Muir Wilderness and, behind you, the resort town of Mammoth Lakes and U.S. 395. Another 1.4 miles and you're at the lakes.

REST STOPS: There are lovely primitive campsites along the way and at the lakes. There's another great one about halfway on the drive, in a pretty aspen grove with Laurel Creek running through. Mammoth Lakes has all the amenities. Try its annual Jazz Jubilee in July, Devil's Postpile National Monument west of town, and the Hot Creek geologic site, 3 miles east of U.S. 395 on Owens River Road. At the Hot Creek Fish Hatchery, open to the public daily, geothermally heated water mixes with cold water from Mammoth Creek to create an ideal environment for raising fish. To get there, drive south on U.S. 395 for 3 miles, then turn east at the airport turnoff. Drive another 0.9 mile and follow the signs.

GETTING HOME: Backtrack to U.S. 395.

MAP: Inyo National Forest.

INFORMATION: Mammoth Ranger Station, (619) 924–5500; Mammoth Lakes Visitors Bureau, (619) 934–2712.

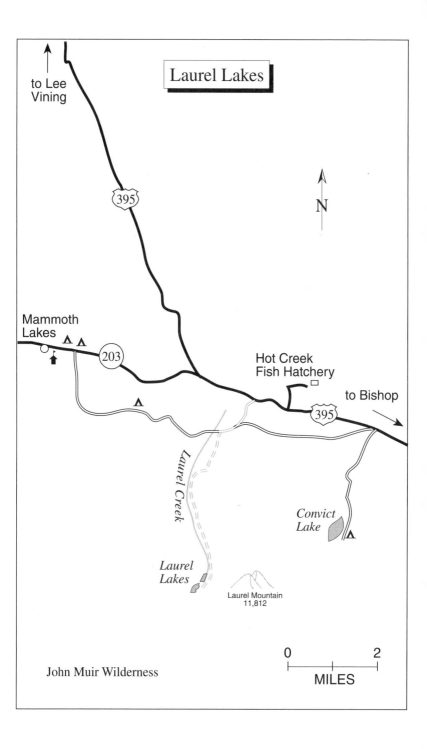

Laurel Lakes

to Lee Vining

to Bishop

Mammoth Lakes

Hot Creek Fish Hatchery

Laurel Creek

Convict Lake

Laurel Lakes

Laurel Mountain 11,812

John Muir Wilderness

0   2
MILES

Middle Palisade Glacier and Southfork Pass from Coyote Flat.

The Sierras, looking west from the White Mountains.

TRIP
31

Coyote Flat

LOCATION: Inyo County southwest of Bishop.

HIGHLIGHTS: A variety of terrain and geologic features, from the desert Owens Valley to meadows and glaciers, including Middle Palisade Glacier and Palisade Glacier, the southernmost active glacier in the United States and the largest still in existence in the Sierra. Great hiking, lake fishing. The descent from over 10,000 feet to Bishop 5,800 feet below is stunning.

DIFFICULTY: Easy to moderate. Narrow, rocky spots.

TIME & DISTANCE: About 7.5 hours and 55 miles.

GETTING THERE: From downtown Bishop, take West Line Street west for 1.5 miles. Turn left onto Barlow Lane, then turn right onto Underwood Lane. After 0.8 mile, where the road curves to the right, go left. Set your odometer to 0. Veer right just before the power substation. Go under the power lines.

THE DRIVE: You'll start out on a sandy road. Pass through a ravine, then climb toward a canyon. At 3.9 miles you'll see a branch to the right. Keep left. Go up some switchbacks. Things will get steep and rocky. You'll climb through small canyons strewn with granitic boulders and pinyon pines. You'll pass a branch on the left at 10 miles; continue on the main road. At 12.1 miles you'll reach the left fork to Coyote Flat. You'll return to this; go straight. At 14.6 is the left fork to tiny Coyote Lake; continue on, keeping right. At the next fork you can go left to a beautiful basin, well over 10,000 feet at the base of Coyote Ridge (the road soon becomes too rough) or right along the west shoulder of 11,261–foot Lookout Mountain. At the Coyote Flat turnoff there's a tricky stream crossing. The road beyond is easy with views of glacier–carved peaks and terminal moraines. You'll pass an airstrip used to test Army helicopters. The glacier to the southwest is Middle Palisade. About 1.2 miles beyond the airstrip you'll reach a left turn to Sugarloaf peak. Take it about 1.6 miles, then veer left again. Follow this track to a viewpoint that provides an outstanding panoramic view and a glimpse of Palisade Glacier. Backtrack to the main road, which ends in a grove of trees with primitive camping and a great view.

REST STOPS: Anywhere along the drive. Visit the Laws Railroad Museum, 4 miles north of Bishop on U.S. Highway 6, and the Paiute Shoshone Indian Cultural Center.

GETTING HOME: Via Bishop and U.S. 395.

MAP: Inyo National Forest.

INFORMATION: White Mountain District, (619) 873–2500. Bishop Chamber of Commerce, (619) 873–8405.

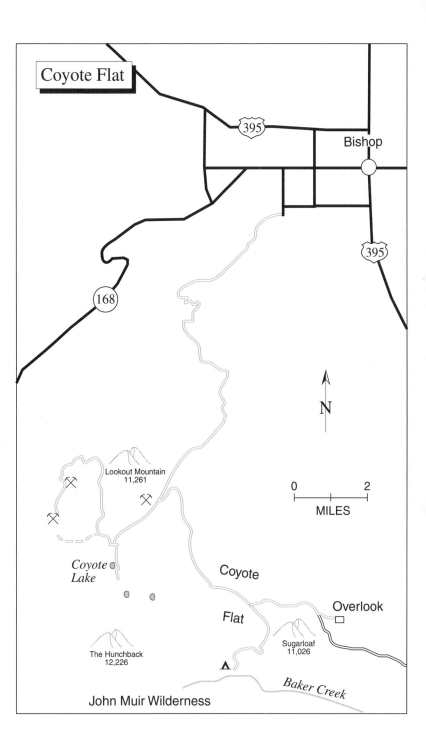

Coyote Flat

395

Bishop

395

168

N

Lookout Mountain
11,261

0   2
MILES

Coyote

Coyote
Lake

Overlook

Flat

The Hunchback
12,226

Sugarloaf
11,026

Baker Creek

John Muir Wilderness

White Mountain Peak.

The White Mountains Loop.

White Mountains Loop

LOCATION: Inyo and Mono counties; east of Bishop and the Owens Valley.

HIGHLIGHTS: The Ancient Bristlecone Pine Forest, whose trees are the oldest living things on Earth; California's third–highest peak, White Mountain Peak (14,246 ft.) in the state's second–highest mountain range; sweeping vistas of the Sierra Nevada; motoring up to 11,650 feet. A crown jewel.

DIFFICULTY: Easy. Moderate and exhilarating if you go up steep and twisting Silver Canyon Road, a route for experienced backcountry motorists. Or you can take the easy paved road up and enjoy the wonderful dirt routes along the crest. There is no water, so bring some cold drinks.

TIME & DISTANCE: A day. About 90 miles round–trip from Bishop via Silver Canyon. Can be taken in either direction.

GETTING THERE: About 3.8 miles north of Bishop on U.S. Highway 6, turn east onto Silver Canyon Road. If you would rather take the easy but beautiful paved road up, go south 15 miles on U.S. 395 toward Big Pine. Turn northeast on Highway 168. After 12.7 miles turn north on White Mountain Road.

THE DRIVE: At the top, you'll travel on good dirt roads among rolling mountaintops and through high valleys, passing rare western bristlecone pines that are thousands of years old. While the Silver Canyon route is a fascinating geologic experience, and really not difficult, it is a very steep climb on a narrow mountainside road. Beginners should think twice. Anyway, you'll start at 4,140 feet in Bishop and end up at 11,650 feet at the trailhead leading to a University of California research center and the summit of White Mountain Peak, a 7.5–mile hike.

REST STOPS: Visit the Laws Railroad Museum 4 miles north of Bishop, off Highway 6, and the Paiute Shoshone Indian Cultural Center in Bishop, a mile west of U.S. 395 on West Line Street. Grandview campground is about 5 miles north of Highway 68 on the White Mountain Road. Schulman Grove has the oldest known bristlecones in the world, a small visitors center and a picnic area. Patriarch Grove has the largest known bristlecone. Try Bishop's Labor Day Wild West Weekend. For food, try The Pyrenees, Firehouse Grill or Roberto's Cafe.

GETTING HOME: U.S. 395 north or south.

MAP: Inyo National Forest.

INFORMATION: White Mountain Ranger Station, (619) 873–2500; Bishop Chamber of Commerce, (619) 873–8405.

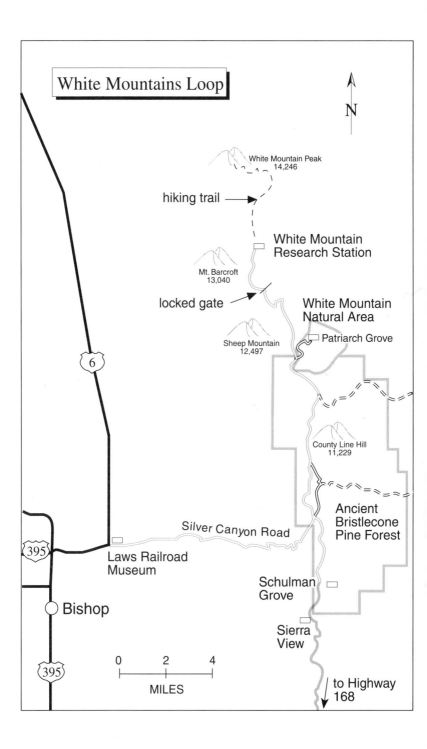

White Mountains Loop

N

White Mountain Peak
14,246

hiking trail ➤

White Mountain
Research Station

Mt. Barcroft
13,040

locked gate ➤

White Mountain
Natural Area

6

Sheep Mountain
12,497

Patriarch Grove

County Line Hill
11,229

Silver Canyon Road

Ancient
Bristlecone
Pine Forest

395

Laws Railroad
Museum

Schulman
Grove

◯ Bishop

Sierra
View

395

0   2   4

MILES

to Highway
168

APPENDIX

Forest Service signs

The boundary of travel restricted areas may be marked as shown below; also refer to road, trail and area restrictions on maps:

Other signs you may encounter are:

 Two-wheel motor vehicle

 Sedan

 High clearance vehicle 4X4 and pickup

 All-terrain vehicle

 Snowmobile

 Symbol with red slash indicates activity not allowed. Symbol with Yellow slash indicates activity not recommended.

 Bicycles

National Forest route markers

Travel management poster

 Roads maintained for low-clearance vehicles, such as sedans, trailers and motorhomes.

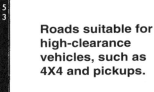 **Roads suitable for high-clearance vehicles, such as 4X4 and pickups.**

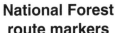

Refer to Forest Service maps for specific vehicle and route designations.

Source: U.S. Forest Service

Sources of information

Bishop Chamber of Commerce
690 N. Main Street
Bishop, CA 93514
(619) 873–8405

Bodie State Historic Park
P.O. Box 515
Bridgeport, CA 93517
(619) 647–6445

Bureau of Land Management;
Bishop Resource Area
787 Main St., Suite P
Bishop, CA 93514
(619) 872–4881

California Association of
Four–Wheel Drive Clubs
3104 O Street #313
Sacramento, CA 95816
(916) 332–8890

Devil's Postpile National
Monument
P.O. Box 501
Mammoth Lakes, CA 93546
(619) 934–2289

Eastern Sierra InterAgency
Visitor Center
At the intersection of state
Highway 136 & U.S. 395
P.O. Drawer R
Lone Pine, CA 93545
(619) 876–4252

Eldorado National Forest
Information Center
3070 Camino Heights Drive
Camino, CA 95709
(916) 644–6048

Eldorado National Forest
Amador Ranger District
26820 Silver Drive & state
Highway 88
Star Route 3
Pioneer, CA 95666
(209) 295–4251

Inyo National Forest
Mammoth District
P.O. Box 148
Mammoth Lakes, CA 93546
(619) 924–5500
Visitors center is on the north side
of Highway 203 just east of down-
town and about 3 miles west of
U.S. 395

Inyo National Forest
Mono Lake District
Along Tioga Road west of U.S.
395
P.O. Box 429
Lee Vining, CA 93541
(619) 647–6525

Inyo National Forest
White Mountain District
798 N. Main Street
Bishop, CA 93514
(619) 873–2500

Lake Tahoe Basin Management
Unit (U.S. Forest Service)
870 Emerald Bay Road
Box 731002
South Lake Tahoe, CA
95731–7302
(916) 573–2600

**Lake Tahoe Forest Service
Visitor Information Center**
On state Highway 89 between
Emerald Bay and South Lake
Tahoe
870 Emerald Bay Road
Suite 1
South Lake Tahoe, CA 96150
(916) 573–2674

**Laws Railroad Museum and
Historical Site**
P.O. Box 363
Bishop, CA 93514
(619) 873–5950

**Mammoth Lakes Visitors
Bureau**
Village Center Mall West
P.O. Box 48
Mammoth Lakes, CA 93546
(619) 934–2712

**Mono Basin National Forest
Scenic Area Visitors Center**
Just north of Lee Vining on U.S.
395; overlooks Mono Lake.
(619) 647–6572

**Mono Lake Committee
Information Center &
Bookstore; Lee Vining Chamber
of Commerce**
Located in the center of town in
Lee Vining on U.S. 395.
P.O. Box 29
Lee Vining, CA 93541
(619) 647–6595

**Paiute Shoshone Indian Cultural
Center**
P.O. Box 1281
Bishop, CA 93515
(619) 873–4478

Stanislaus National Forest
Calaveras Ranger District
State Highway 4
P.O. Box 500
Hathaway Pines, CA 95232
(209) 795–1381

Tahoe National Forest
Nevada City Ranger District
12012 Sutton Way
Grass Valley, CA 95945
(916) 265–4531

Tahoe National Forest
Sierraville Ranger District
Sierraville, CA 96126
(916) 994–3401

Toiyabe National Forest
Carson Ranger District
1536 S. Carson Street
Carson City, NV 89701
(702) 882–2766

Toiyabe National Forest
Bridgeport Ranger District
P.O. Box 595
Bridgeport, CA 93517
(619) 932–7070

Tread Lightly!, Inc.
298 24th Street
Suite 325–C
Ogden, Utah 84401
(801) 627–0077
1–800–966–9900

U.S. Forest Service
Camping reservations
1–800–283–CAMP

Index

PHOTO INDEX

Trip notes